Help, We're Having a Baby

H. NORMAN WRIGHT
MARVIN N. INMON

Regal Books

A Division of GL Publications
Ventura, CA U.S.A.

Other books by H. Norman Wright
Communication: Key to Your Marriage
More Communication Keys for Your Marriage
The Pillars of Marriage
Seasons of a Marriage
So You're Getting Married

Rights for publishing this book in other languages are contracted by Gospel Literature International (GLINT) foundation. GLINT also provides technical help for
the adaptation, translation, and publishing of Bible study resources and books in
scores of languages worldwide. For further information, contact GLINT, Post
Office Box 6688, Ventura, California 93006, U.S.A., or the publisher.

Scripture quotations in this publication, unless otherwise noted, are from the *New
American Standard Bible.* © The Lockman Foundation 1960, 1962, 1963, 1968,
1971, 1972, 1973, 1975. Used by permission. Other versions quoted include:
NIV—New International Version, Holy Bible. Copyright © 1978 by New York
International Bible Society. Used by permission.
AMP—The Amplified Bible, Copyright 1962, 1964, 1965 by Zondervan Publish-
ing House. Used by permission.
TLB—The Living Bible, Copyright © 1971 by Tyndale House Publishers,
Wheaton, Illinois. Used by permission.
KJV—The Authorized King James Version.
RSV—Revised Standard Version of the Bible, copyrighted 1946 and 1952 by the
Division of Christian Education of the NCCC, U.S.A., and used by permission.

Previously published under the title *Preparing for Parenthood*

Third Printing, 1986

Publishing by Regal Books
A Division of GL Publications
Ventura, California 93006
Printed in U.S.A.

Library of Congress Catalog Card No. 79-92949
ISBN 0-8307-0743-3

Contents

A Leader's Guide for use with this book is
available from your church supplier.

To Be or Not to Be—Parents

We arrived home at 11:00. The wedding of my wife's best friend had been enjoyable. Joyce was scheduled to be part of that wedding but where do you find a bridesmaid's dress to fit someone who is eight months and 29 days pregnant!

So we were spectators. All during the ceremony Joyce kept checking her watch as though she were timing something. As we drove home she announced, "I think we're in for a long night. Someone may be going to announce his presence." Three hours after we came home we left for the hospital. The vigil began at 3:00 A.M. Then we waited and waited and waited. I sat with Joyce and we counted the minutes between contractions. We talked and waited. After 16 hours and numerous trips to the snack shop and reading every magazine in sight, Joyce was taken to the delivery room. One minute we were just a married couple. The next minute we were instant parents, ready or not. I didn't feel like a parent! I really didn't know what to do as a parent. I guess my big question was, now what?

When *you* think "parent," what other words or images come to mind? A myriad of terms have been used to describe parenthood, including "a test of endurance," "ultimate fulfillment," and "a job from which no one can fire you.'' The word *parent*, according to most dictionaries, means ''a father or mother'' and carries with it the connotation of ''one who begets or brings forth offspring.'' Parenthood is more, however, than procreation and instinctual behavior. Parenthood involves psychological and spiritual aspects along with the biological. The assumption that the ability to parent is instinctual just as the ability to give birth is false. The ability to parent does not come naturally. It requires careful planning, hard work, and much patience.

Being a parent is like being an astronaut, said the authors of *The Parent Test*. ''No matter how much you are told, how much training and instruction you receive, your own experience can't really be predicted: It will be new, uncharted, uniquely yours. Being a parent is also akin to being a nurse or doctor, because of the patience and selflessness required (and the long hours)! Being a parent is somewhat like being a teacher, too, since you continually need to impart knowledge, evaluate learning, and hold eventual 'graduation' in sight.

''Parenthood is a little like all these occupations.

''And it's a little like swimming.

''Some people plunge in without thinking and do a beautiful breast stroke; others just barely manage a 'survival float'; and still others can't manage even *that* and have to call for help. Some wait until the hottest day of summer and even then test the water carefully to the ankle prior to a more deliberate immersion; others will swim in any season (and some simply won't go near the water).''[1]

Expectations of Parents

When you dream about children and being a parent, you fantasize about yourself and your child to be. You dream about the type of parent you want to be and the type of child you want to have. Fantasizing is normal; but are the images you see in your dreams realistic? Are they only wishful or are they grounded in realistic expectations? Do these dreams help you fulfill your wishes?

We have high expectations of ourselves as parents, and others have high expectations of us, too. Sometimes these expectations are so high that we are expected to rear children who are ''better'' than we. "This is a sobering thought," said E.E. LeMasters, who is known for his research with young parents. "It will not be enough for the parents to produce carbon copies of themselves; they will have to do what some of the new copying machines are supposed to do—turn out copies better than the originals.

"It would seem that this is one of the reasons why modern parents feel so inadequate. They are not sure they are able to do what is required. And their children are not sure either."[2]

Rather than trying to determine what the ideal parent is from our own limited perspectives or what we think society expects of us as parents, we should conform to God's design for parenthood. Parenthood is involved in the creation of new life, so we need to understand the purpose of creation.

God created the universe to show His glory and character, as we learn from Isaiah the prophet: "I will say to the north, 'Give them up!' And to the south, 'Do not hold them back.' Bring My sons from afar, and My daughters from the ends of the earth, every one who is called by My name, and whom I have created for My glory, whom I have formed even whom I have made" (Isa. 43:6,7).

God wants mankind to reflect this glory.

Bruce Narramore related the purpose of reflecting God's glory to the purpose of the family in these words: "If God's purpose is to communicate His glory through creation, then the primary purpose of the family is to be a vehicle in this process. And if the family is to communicate God's glory, family members must be experiencing that glory. In other words, the family should be instrumental in promoting righteousness among its members because God is glorified when His character is reproduced in His children."[3] One of the purposes of parenting, then, is to *help a child's character reflect God's glory.*

A second purpose of parenthood is seen in Genesis 1:28: "And God blessed them; and God said to them, 'Be fruitful and multiply, and fill the earth, and subdue it; and rule over the fish of the sea and over the birds of the sky, and over every living thing that moves on the earth.'" *God has asked us to replenish the earth.*

A third purpose of parenthood is seen in Psalm 127:3-5, where children are described as "a gift of the Lord," "a reward," and "arrows" in a man's quiver. *We are to enjoy our children.*

God also uses parenthood to *teach us about Himself*. "The point is well established in the Bible," said Richard Strauss, author of *Confident Children and How They Grow*. "God's parenthood and our parenthood are a great deal alike—at least they should be. . . . A person's image of God is often patterned after his image of his own parents, especially his father. If his parents were happy, loving, accepting, and forgiving, he finds it easier to experience a positive and satisfying relationship with God. But if his parents were cold and indifferent, he may feel that God is far away and disinterested in him personally. If his parents were angry, hostile, and rejecting he often feels that God can never accept him. If his parents were hard to please, he usually has the nagging notion that God is not very happy with him either."[4]

Yet another purpose of parenthood is *teaching, nurturing, and training our children*. "And you shall teach them [the words of the Lord] diligently to your sons and shall talk of them when you sit in your house and when you walk by the way and when you lie down and when you rise up" (Deut. 6:7). "And, fathers, do not provoke your children to anger; but bring them up in the discipline and instruction of the Lord" (Eph. 6:4). "Train up a child in the way he should go, even when he is old he will not depart from it" (Prov. 22:6).

This purpose—to teach and to train—is seen also in the following Scriptures, where parents are:
- to be an example (1 Kings 9:4; 2 Chron. 17:3)
- to provide for (2 Cor. 12:14)
- to control (1 Tim. 3:4)
- to love (Titus 2:4)
- to correct (Prov. 13:24; 19:18; 22:15; 23:13).

WHAT DO YOU THINK?

1. List 10 indications that now is the time of your life to have children.

(1)

(2)

   (3)

   (4)

   (5)

   (6)

   (7)

   (8)

   (9)

   (10)

2. If you were brought before a jury to convince them that you are worthy of being a parent, what would you say?

3. What changes will occur in your life-style when you become a parent?

Joys of Parenthood

Parenthood holds potential for growth and delight. The delight of parenthood comes from doing for our child *and* growing personally at the same time. Our task as parents is more than creating and molding a child. If we focus only on his growth, what happens to *our* growth? If a parent stagnates, what can he give to a child? A growing and maturing parent has the most to give to a child.

This philosophy of parenthood as part of the life process of personal development is not popular. "There are very strong cultural influences in the United States that value the care of the young above the needs of adults. Adults are viewed as being ideal, as 'rugged individualists,' as not having needs. Their behavior patterns are thought to be final, established, unchanging. Children and adolescents are expected to go through a number of developmental stages, but once they reach adulthood many people think their development is finished. The adult is supposed to stay basically the same in his thinking and needs and responses, at least until he reaches middle age and has to develop new directions for his life—and by this time his children are usually mature, so he is no longer an active parent. These views are not accurate," stated the Committee on Public Education Group for the Advancement of Psychiatry. "Parents are not just 'vehicles' for the care of children. They are people, and parenthood is one phase in their total development as human beings, a development that never stops but continues from birth to death."[5]

As Christians we are to be continually maturing and growing. Family life should not be an anchor, hindering progress. Being realistic about the complexities of parenthood and preparing for them will relieve many of our anxieties and resolve many future problems. Our joy can come from this new life given from the Creator of life.

Excitement, relief, and gladness are immediate results of giving birth. The apostle John described this excitement with Jesus' words of assurance to His disciples: "Truly, truly, I say to you, that you will weep and lament, but the world will rejoice; you will be sorrowful, but your sorrow will be turned to joy. Whenever a woman is in travail she has sorrow, because her hour has come; but when she gives birth to the child, she remembers the anguish no more, for joy that a child has been born into the world. Therefore you, too, now have sorrow; but I will see you again, and your heart will rejoice, and no one takes your joy away from you" (John 16:20-22).

WHAT DO YOU THINK?

1. What are your feelings (or your spouse's) about what has just been said?

2. What words describe your marriage at the present time?

Pressures, Demands, and Conflicts

There are no guarantees in parenting. There are no formulas to follow that are guaranteed to develop good character and personality in a child. Furthermore, the end result of all our thinking, effort, and sacrifice in parenting cannot be measured for at least a decade or more, although we must make instantaneous decisions on many occasions.

When a child is born, the identities of both parents are tested. Husbands and wives by this time have found ways to build their identities through success in certain performance-oriented tasks, jobs, or skills. When the child arrives, the qualities we feel we possess are soon tested. If we are successful in this new venture, we are satisfied that we have made a wise decision. But if either the results are negative or our anticipated needs are not fulfilled through parenthood, our identity may suffer. If we depend on positive feedback concerning our role as a parent and it doesn't come, our self-esteem may begin to diminish.

A child places verbal and nonverbal demands upon parents' time, and we soon learn that time does not belong to us any longer. With the first (and even the second) child, the often-repeated dilemma of not knowing what to do for the child arouses guilt and anxiety. Parents must exhibit tremendous control in all situations because children have frequent lapses of control.

Responding to a child is different than responding to people in the career world where there are definite and specific guidelines for communication. There the end result of communication in many cases is immediate and there is equal and free communication between adults. When a child is involved, especially a very young child, a parent's confidence in knowing how to handle situations can erode.

Picture yourself in the bind of many formerly employed mothers. You have had a degree of independence and accomplishment in your job. Now you have exchanged your job for motherhood, which may involve insecurity, indecisiveness, and little assurance that what you are doing is best. What happens to the feelings of competence you once had when you were employed? These feelings may begin to diminish, and your ability to accomplish anything may seem to diminish also. Thus your identity begins to erode. Many mothers and (most) fathers are now aware of this. The husband's support and involvement definitely act as a stable force during this time.

Having a child has the effect of making a woman become selfless and more concerned about the care of another than she was before. To some degree she must rely more on her husband than before. As she takes care of another, she needs to be taken care of herself, whether she wants to be or not. In a healthy relationship this need has little or no lessening effect on one's sense of identity.

The pressures on mother are evident in many ways. Roger Gould, M.D., described these pressures in his book *Transformations:* "In her daily experience with a child, a mother's time is not her own. She has to respond constantly to unclear verbal and preverbal demands from her child. Often she has no idea what to do; many times no good solution is available, so she'll suffer guilt and anxiety no matter what she does. The child constantly explores the boundaries of her patience and power. When the child's control lapses, her own control is required. She must consider using force on a helpless human being who sometimes invades her bodily privacy and psychological integrity like a monstrous, consuming enemy. She deals with the world of child rearing, where hundreds of experts give contradictory advice; the outcome can't be measured for fifteen to twenty years. She has to process this advice through her intuition and a constant stream of her own childhood memories dredged up by her child's dilemmas. And she must do all this with others—mother, mother-in-law, neighbors and school teachers—looking over her shoulder, marking her report card, measuring her against their own standards. Though it would be a relief to give up and follow some set of packaged rules, she must dare to be different—the fate of her child depends on her decisions. Besides, no set of rules seems exactly right."[6]

At this time in her life, a mother experiences a wide range of varied and contrasting emotions. Feelings vary from joy to terror about being pregnant, from anxiety over the impending birth to delightful discussion over the selection of a name for the newborn. There are days of abounding energy and others of extreme fatigue.

The new role of motherhood often does away with some of her own wishes and desires, which she can no longer pursue. "Abandon yourself for the good of another" is the maxim she has heard from her parents, church, or friends. Following this advice she encounters conflict, for in not meeting her own needs and wishes sufficiently, she has less to give to the child and her fear of being a "bad mother" intensifies.

Dr. Gould described this process in detail: "After giving birth, women experience the child as part of their psychological self. They merge with it and develop an uncanny ability to respond to its changes. It is a deep connection that no man can really share, just as no man can experience a live child growing within his body and being nourished by the nutrients that are carried in his blood. A child is part of the mother's flesh and blood even outside her body.

"This normal and necessary symbiosis of early motherhood rekindles a woman's unconscious symbiotic experience with her own mother. Her earliest and most enduring love attachments were with her mother. Having a baby expresses more than a biological urge or love of a husband or a desire to create; it is a bedrock tie to a woman's femaleness—and to the mother who gave birth to her.

"A girl's childhood model of the ideal mother becomes her operating criterion for being a good mother in adulthood. The ideal mother met all of her needs and wishes, was always there to comfort her, never let her be in danger, saw to it that she had every pleasure, and never left her out by choosing to be with friends or husband. The ideal mother was *selfless,* devoted to the child's welfare and ease of living, and had no life of her own; or if she did, she would abandon it without a moment's hesitation when the child wanted something."[7]

Many mothers feel socially deprived because they carry too

much of the responsibility for the child. Because of this constant giving and suppression of her own needs, a sensitive husband who can give an abundance of love and attention to his wife is a necessity. The husband and wife who share in the rearing activities find that their intimacy quotient can remain high and grow in a new direction. The partnership helps the mother overcome the common feeling of "I cannot grow and develop anymore because of give, give, give!" Sharing responsibility frees her to grow and she can perhaps realize that the adventure of parenthood is also a tremendous avenue of growth.

Prior to the arrival of the first child, many couples enjoy their marriage relationship as equals. This balance has resulted in a healthy intimacy. In an equal relationship, intimacy has the best opportunity to develop.

In what way do you anticipate parenthood affecting your marriage? positively, negatively, or not at all? Consider these findings:

"In 1974 the Institute for Social Research found that the periods of greatest satisfaction for parents were (1) the years before they had children; (2) the years after the children left home!

"In 1975 the International Health Foundation in Geneva declared the childless marriage to be more stable, more healthy. Dr. Pieter Van Keep, the foundation's director, said, 'Young children frequently interfere with communication, and communication is vital to marital harmony.'

"The birth of a baby seems to catalyze (though probably not cause) stresses, difficulties, and transitions for the parents. Four researchers recently studied 14 expectant couples in the San Francisco area from mid-pregnancy through the period approximately six months after birth. Some of their findings are as follows: all couples noted radical changes in self-esteem, marital communication, and work roles; changes in self-image for both parents were more in a negative than positive direction; all of the fathers had a 'career crisis' as the birth of the child approached; all couples reported a short-lived emotional 'high' following birth; regardless of division of work before the birth of the baby, after birth it shifted to a traditional division, particularly regarding household chores, but also in family decision-making roles and baby care; initiating sexual activity became increasingly a male task; none of the couples accurately anticipated changes in amounts of leisure time as a result of having a baby in the family; parenting attitudes and philosophies changed dramatically after the baby was actually present; all couples reported significant shifts in their communication patterns."[8]

Most other studies indicate that of those participating in these surveys, newly married couples have high marital satisfaction which decreases prior to and after the first child. There appears to be a crisis during the birth of the other children as well. These crises vary in intensity from slight to severe. Along with the crises, feelings of delight and elation exist.

Crises do not have to be destructive or cause marital satisfaction to diminish. If couples are aware of the adjustments and stresses and can work together, the birth of a child can be a rich time of both individual and marital growth. Research shows that the stronger the marriage is prior to parenthood, the fewer the problems; and the more time a couple has alone in the evening to work on their marriage, the fewer the complaints."[9]

WHAT DO YOU THINK?

Answer the following questions and see if you want to be or not to be parents.[10] Ask your spouse to answer these questions then discuss them together.

Does having and raising a child fit the life-style I want?
1. What do I want out of life for myself? What do I think is important?

2. Could I handle a child and a job at the same time? Would I have time and energy for both?

3. Would I be ready to give up the freedom to do what I want to do, when I want to do it?

4. Would I be willing to cut back my social life and spend more time at home? Would I miss my free time and privacy?

5. Can I afford to support a child? Do I know how much it takes to raise a child?

6. Do I want to raise a child in the neighborhood where I live now? Would I be willing and able to move?

7. How would a child interfere with my growth and development?

8. Would a child change my educational plans? Do I have the energy to go to school and raise a child at the same time?

9. Am I willing to give a great part of my life—at least 18 years—to being responsible for a child? And spend a large portion of my life being concerned about my child's well-being?

What's in it for me?
10. Do I like doing things with children? Do I enjoy activities that children can do?

11. Would I want a child to be "like me"?

12. Would I try to pass on to my child my ideas and values? What if my child's ideas and values turn out to be different from mine?

13. Would I want my child to achieve things that I wish I had but didn't?

14. Would I expect my child to keep me from being lonely in my old age? Do I do that for my parents? Do my parents do that for my grandparents?

15. Do I want a boy or a girl child? What if I don't get what I want?

16. Would having a child show others how mature I am?

17. Will I prove I am a man or a woman by having a child?

18. Do I expect my child to make my life happy?

Raising a child—what's there to know?
19. Do I like children? When I'm around children for awhile, what do I think or feel about having one around all of the time?

20. Do I enjoy teaching others?

21. Is it easy for me to tell other people what I want or what I expect of them?

22. Do I want to give a child the love he or she needs? Is loving easy for me?

23. Am I patient enough to deal with the noise and the confusion and the 24-hour-a-day responsibility? What kind of time and space do I need for myself?

24. What do I do when I get angry or upset? Would I take things out on a child if I lost my temper?

25. What does discipline mean to me? What does freedom, or setting limits, or giving space mean? What is being too strict or not strict enough? Would I want a perfect child?

26. How do I get along with my parents? What will I do to avoid the mistakes my parents made?

27. How would I take care of my child's health and safety? How do I take care of my own?

28. What if I have a child and find out I made a wrong decision?

Have my partner and I really talked about becoming parents?
29. Does my partner want to have a child? Have we talked about our reasons?

30. Could we give a child a good home? Is our relationship a happy and strong one?

31. Are we both ready to give our time and energy to raising a child?

32. Could we share our love with a child without jealousy?

33. What would happen if we separated after having a child or if one of us should die?

34. Do my partner and I understand each other's feelings about religion, work, family, child-rearing, future goals? Do we feel pretty much the same way? Will children fit into these feelings, hopes and plans?

35. Suppose one of us wants a child and the other doesn't? Who decides?

Motives for Parenthood

The authors of *The Parent Test* suggested four categories of motives for becoming a parent. The first is *egotistic*. Examples they list of clearly egotistic reasons for wanting children include:
- to have a child who will look like me
- to have a child who will carry on my admirable traits
- to have a child who will be successful
- to have someone who will carry on my name
- to inherit family money or property
- to have someone who will regard me as the greatest
- to do something that I know I could do well
- to feel the pride of creation
- to keep me young in heart
- to help me feel fulfilled.

Some motives are *compensatory* in nature:
- to make my marriage happier

- to make up for my own unhappy family background
- to make up for lack of satisfaction in my job
- to make up for social isolation, lack of friends
- to make me feel more secure about my masculinity/femininity.

These compensatory motives are especially dangerous. Many couples think that children will help solve their problems. Many couples want children to "save" their marriage. If a marriage needs saving, asking a baby to do it is asking a person for skills he or she doesn't possess. A baby's presence could even distract the couple from analyzing and correcting their difficulties. Having a baby to save a bad marriage only makes the marriage worse! The same applies to having a baby for solving other problems.

Conforming motives include:
- to be like most other people
- to please my parents
- to forestall social criticism.

Although not as seriously dangerous as compensatory motives, conforming motives are poor reasons for becoming a parent because the desire is not to have a child but to please someone else.

Affectionate motives include:
- to have a real opportunity to make someone happy
- to teach someone about all the beautiful things in life
- to have the satisfaction of giving myself to someone else
- to help someone grow and develop.

These are good reasons for wanting to become a parent.

WHAT DO YOU THINK?

1. Which of these motives have you felt at one time or another?

2. Of the motives that you have felt, which are healthy? Which are not?

3. What do you feel are Christian-oriented motives for having children?

Another reason many people become parents is not really a motive for making a decision to become a parent. It could be called decision by *default* or *accident*. Nathan B. Talbot, M.D., discusses the results of unwanted or "surprise" pregnancies in *Raising Children in Modern America:* "One of the most extreme untoward results of unwanted pregnancies is child abuse—a growing phenomenon. The trouble here stems from the fact that children, being human, are not always easy to live with. When they get hurt or hungry or frustrated it is natural for them to fret or cry or lose their tempers, and at times this can try the patience of even the calmest parent. On such occasions it helps greatly to have chosen to take on the responsibilities of child-rearing. Unfortunately, these are the moments when a parent who did not want a child in the first place feels overwhelmed and may break down and vent his or her pent-up feelings of frustration and anger by brutalizing a youngster who not only may be totally helpless but also quite innocent of any serious misdeeds.[11]

Preparing for Parenthood

Survival and fulfillment as a parent depend on many factors, one of which is adequate preparation. Part of the process of preparation is being creative enough to learn through the experience and resources of other competent parents. Susan Isaacs and Marti Keller, authors of *The Inner Parent,* discuss the process of learning from others:

"Parents who have prepared for childbirth are often hit with three realizations immediately after the birth of their child: (1) that if they have been prepared for childbirth, they have been grossly underprepared for parenthood; (2) that the relationships and sharing they experienced in their preparatory childbirth classes now seem as valuable as the content of those classes; (3) that if they saw, in childbirth, that they could have some control over the process, why shouldn't that self-determination continue?

"The first realization describes an initial crisis of parenting. The second and third are the basis for some of the avenues that modern parents are beginning to explore in order to fulfill their own unique potentials as persons who are parents.

"Today more and more parents are attempting to discover what it is *they* believe through an examination of their perceptions, both alone and in the supportive presence of others. They are learning to discover and implement their own values. They are creating and attending groups in their homes, schools, churches, and elsewhere as forums where they can discuss their feelings about children and about how being a parent has changed their feelings toward themselves."12

Although preparation for parenthood is important, it is almost nonexistent. Schools are very deficient in the topics that are so necessary for this important role. Most couples who experience any preparation at all for parenthood do so minimally during the nine months of pregnancy, and most mothers do more reading and discussing than fathers.

When the stage of parenthood finally arrives it does so with an abrupt and sudden onset. We spend many years preparing for our vocation and in some instances work into it gradually. We spend six months to four years becoming acquainted with our spouse prior to marriage and this relationship gradually grows and develops. Not so with parenthood! We are aware that the child is coming, and then abruptly—a minute later—this new stranger is alive, loud and demanding.

As I said at the beginning of this chapter, the night before our first child's birth, my wife Joyce and I went out for the evening to a close friend's wedding. We didn't have to be concerned about a baby-sitter that evening. We ate dinner when we wanted, left the house as planned, stopped after the wedding to visit and eat, and retired for the evening when we chose. At 1:00 A.M. our daughter began to clamor for release. This was the first of many intrusions and demands upon our lives.

As I write this book, Joyce and I are two weeks into the next stage of our passage through our adult lives, the empty nest. Sheryl is at college. Have 18 years fled by so fast? How we have grown during this time! As she left, part of us was encouraging, gently pushing her from the nest to spread her own wings which she so eagerly had been testing and using. Another part of us continued to cling, for the act of releasing is not always easy. There is a sense of loss, loneliness, and the feeling "What more can we do to help her grow? Have we done all we can?" The answer is no. But that's all right, too. Every child will have much to discover and learn on his own without his parents.

The day after she left for college with her belongings, I walked into her room and sat for awhile. I experienced two reactions: (1) this is the cleanest and neatest I've ever seen her room in years; (2) the room is also empty. It was a new type of emptiness I'd never felt before. For a moment I preferred it the other way. You see, when a child leaves you experience a mixture of feelings. When a child enters your life you will also have a mixture of feelings. Relax, for all of these feelings are normal.

As we look back upon the past 20 years, Joyce and I realize that we have traveled through three of the four phases of parenthood. [13] First, we experienced *anticipation*. Unlike some couples who have looked forward to parenthood since their early years, we thought about it only casually. It was not until Joyce became pregnant that we gave greater thought to what parenthood really means.

We then entered the *honeymoon* phase of parenthood. To say the least, this was a time of adjustment and learning. We had to learn new roles, skills, and new levels of patience and flexibility. As Sheryl grew, we became more and more attached to her.

The next stage in the parental cycle which we experienced has been called the *plateau*. The cycle has been aptly described by David Friedman, M.D.:

"The child is an infant: parents learn to interpret his needs.

"The child is a toddler: parents learn to accept growth and development.

"The child is a preschooler: parents and child learn to separate.

"The child goes to school: parents learn to accept rejection and still be supportive.

"The child is a teenager: parents begin to rebuild their lives." [14]

During the preteen years, parents need to begin the process of deparenting themselves. We struggle to learn the role of parenthood and then must relinquish the role, and that too is a struggle. But one of our parental roles is assisting the child to become an independent, responsible person. And this process must begin when the child is quite young. If we feel confident and secure in ourselves and our own abilities, this task is a bit easier. The preteen years are also the time for parents to begin to rebuild and redirect their own lives as they prepare for the empty nest.

The last stage for Joyce and me is yet to come in its completion. *Disengagement* is a stage leading to the end of the active parental role. This stage is often considered to occur at the time of the child's marriage, but the time varies greatly with the couple. In some ways, we have already experienced this stage with our 13-year-old son, Matthew. He went to live in a special facility for severely retarded individuals in March, 1978. We went through deparenting and disengagement over a period of time before and after he entered, and we continually experience this stage when we bring Matthew home to visit every third weekend. During the following week, we must once again adjust.

Knowing about and anticipating these stages will make the transitions easier for you too.

Before you become a parent, consider the job description and working conditions. Would you apply for a job without asking about the pay, hours, working conditions, time off, co-workers, training opportunities, advancement? Probably not. Yet most parents do not inquire into the details of the task of being a parent.

Too many people who marry and have children are oblivious to the potential dangers of parenthood or feel that the delights will overcome any problems they may encounter. When the needs of a child are met, parents' needs and expectations are met, and society's demands are met. Then a balance is achieved and there is happiness. Problems occur when the needs and expectations conflict. Then the harmonious balance is broken. For many parents, disharmony between them and their child is often the norm rather than the exception.

As with all other decisions in life, we need to seek God's will and ask His guidance. His timing for our lives is most important. He does not require that all married couples become parents. This is a decision to consider carefully through prayer and study.

If you do become a parent, you become a partner in creation—I don't mean just with your spouse, but with God too. He is the giver of life and created both of you in such a manner that you could be involved in procreation.

God knows all about your child before he or she is born, just as

He knows about you: "For Thou didst form my inward parts; Thou didst weave me in my mother's womb. I will give thanks to Thee, for I am fearfully and wonderfully made; wonderful are Thy works, and my soul knows it very well. My frame was not hidden from Thee, when I was made in secret, and skillfully wrought in the depths of the earth. Thine eyes have seen my unformed substance; and in Thy book they were all written, the days that were ordained for me, when as yet there was not one of them" (Ps. 139:13-16).

"Thy hands fashioned and made me altogether, and wouldst Thou destroy me? Remember now, that Thou hast made me as clay; and wouldst Thou turn me into dust again? Didst Thou not pour me out like milk, and curdle me like cheese; clothe me with skin and flesh, and knit me together with bones and sinews? Thou hast granted me life and lovingkindness; and Thy care has preserved my spirit" (Job 10:8-12).

Your child is not your property either. You have been entrusted with his care: "All husbands and wives borrow their children. Our children are not our own. Our children belong to God. He has loaned them to us for a season. Most marriages contain these borrowed jewels. They are not ours to keep but to rear. They are not given to us to mold into our image. They are not given to us so that we can force them to fulfill our lives and thus, in some way, cancel our failure. They are not tools to be used, but souls to be loved."[15]

WHAT'S YOUR PLAN?

1. Describe in detail the steps you will take to prepare for parenthood.

2. Write in detail a prayer of thanksgiving and petition about your new role as a parent.

Notes

All material quoted is used by permission.

1. William Granzig and Ellen Peck, *The Parent Test* (New York: G.P. Putnam's Sons, 1978), p. 19.

2. E.E. LeMasters, *Parents in Modern America* (Homewood, IL: Dorsey Press, 1970), pp. 64,65.

3. Bruce Narramore, *Parenting with Love and Limits* (Grand Rapids: Zondervan Publishing House, 1979), p. 26.

4. Richard Strauss, *Confident Children and How They Grow* (Wheaton: Tyndale House Publishers, 1975), p. 23.

5. Committee on Public Education Group for the Advancement of Psychiatry, *The Joys and Sorrows of Parenthood* (New York: Charles Scribner's Sons, 1973), p. 18.

6. Roger Gould, M.D., *Transformations* (New York: Simon & Schuster, Inc., 1978), p. 100.

7. *Ibid.*, pp. 101,102.

8. Judy MacKintosh, "News from the Field," *Marriage and Family Review*, I, 3 (May/June, 1978), p. 18.

9. Jane Aldous, *Family Careers—Developmental Changes in Families* (New York: John Wiley & Sons, Inc., 1978), pp. 163,169.

10. From the National Organization for Non-Parents, 806 Reisterstown Road, Baltimore, MD 21208. Reprinted by permission.

11. Nathan B. Talbot, M.D., *Raising Children in Modern America* (Boston: Little, Brown & Co., 1976), p. 12.

12. Susan Isaacs and Marti Keller, *The Inner Parent* (New York: Harcourt Brace Jovanovich, Inc., 1979), pp. 12,13.

13. Adapted from *The Joys and Sorrows of Parenthood*, pp. 23,24.

14. David Friedman, M.D., "Parent Development," *California Medicine*, LXXXVI, 1 (1957), pp. 25-28.

15. Thomas C. Short, "Christian Marriage," *Pulpit Digest*, as quoted in Charles R. Swindoll, *You and Your Child* (Nashville: Thomas Nelson, Inc., 1977), pp. 52,53.

What Do You Have to Offer Your Children?

Imagine yourself living in a society that requires couples who want to become parents to apply for the position of parenthood. Suppose you apply and are required to offer proof that any children you bear will be reared in a good home atmosphere. How would your application read? Would you be accepted?

Although our society will not require you to offer such proof before becoming a parent, you should answer the question for yourself: "What do I have to offer a child?" The answer to this question depends primarily on your marital relationship and your potential parenting style.

Let's consider your marriage first. The quality of your marriage will affect the quality of your parenting. What you believe about marriage and what your marriage reflects about you as a person will affect your parenting. What is your marital relationship like at the present time?

The Devitalized Marriage

Let's compare your marriage to five different types of marriage described by sociologists John F. Cuber and Peggy B. Haroff.[1] The first type of marriage, called the *devitalized marriage,* is a placid, half-alive relationship. This marriage is devoid of emotional involvement, so there is neither conflict nor passion. Individuals in this marriage can be thought of as "married singles." They both live as separate a life as possible and still remain married.

The husband provides his wife with money for running the household and leaves the details to her. His time is consumed with his work and hobbies. There is very little bother from his wife concerning the children or the house unless absolutely necessary. Their communication is definitely surface level with no sharing of thoughts *or* feelings. Sexual relationships are routine and almost obligatory. This type of married life is almost an exchange of services. Bed and board are shared, and that's it!

Even marriages that have previously developed into a positive relationship can slip into this style. Many replacements crop up to impede the relationship. Work can be one replacement, especially if the husband is using his performance and involvement at work to enhance his self-concept. The newspaper, television, sports, reading, children, recreation,hobbies, and church are activities that are innocent in themselves but are frequently used as escape avenues, which characterize this style of marriage. Diagram 1 depicts this kind of marriage.

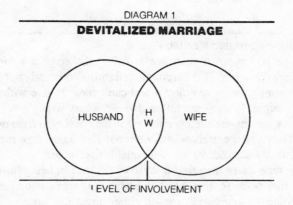

DIAGRAM 1

DEVITALIZED MARRIAGE

HUSBAND   H W   WIFE

LEVEL OF INVOLVEMENT

WHAT DO YOU THINK?

1. What happens to individuals in this type of marriage?

2. What is the probability of this type of marriage staying together? (Circle one): 90 percent, 70 percent, 50 percent, 30 percent, 15 percent.

3. What style of parenting do you think would be reflected by this marriage? (Underline):
   a. Authoritative—balance between discipline and love
   b. Democratic—everyone has a say
   c. Indulgent—parents offer incentives for proper behavior
   d. Authoritarian—parents make the rules
   e. Neglectful—not much attention paid to children
   f. Instructor and guide—parent plays role of a teacher
   g. Permissive—children allowed to do their own thing

4. Describe the kind of family atmosphere you feel this marriage would create for the children.

5. What positive and negative qualities might appear in the children from this type of marriage?

Conflict-Habituated Marriage

A second type of marriage is called the *conflict-habituated marriage* (Diagram 2). This couple is fighting constantly but amazingly enough seems to enjoy it and can't seem to live without it! Often couples like this are referred to as "weary wranglers." Over the years they have developed finesse in their ability to srike out and hurt. They find themselves in a dilemma. They know their methods are basically destructive but seem unable to change.

In some cases they find a sense of comfort in being hostile to each other because then they can blame the other person for their unhappiness. Aggression can be either direct outbursts or subtle forays. Fresh wounds are inflicted before the previous ones have had time to develop protective scabs. The relationship is volatile, but both seem to thrive on it. The involvement level is greater in this marriage but is painful.

DIAGRAM 2

CONFLICT-HABITUATED MARRIAGE

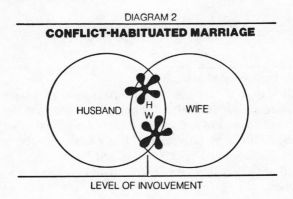

LEVEL OF INVOLVEMENT

WHAT DO YOU THINK?

1. What happens to individuals in this type of marriage?

2. What is the probability of this type of marriage staying together? (Circle one): 90 percent, 70 percent, 50 percent, 30 percent, 15 percent.

3. What style of parenting do you think would be reflected by this marriage? (Underline):
    a. Authoritative—balance between discipline and love
    b. Democratic—everyone has a say
    c. Indulgent—parents offer incentives for proper behavior
    d. Authoritarian—parents make the rules
    e. Neglectful—not much attention paid to children
    f. Instructor and guide—parent plays role of a teacher
    g. Permissive—children allowed to do their own thing

4. Describe the kind of family atmosphere you feel this marriage would create for the children.

5. What positive and negative qualities might appear in the children from this type of marriage?

Passive-Congenial Marriage

A third type of marriage is called the *passive-congenial marriage* (Diagram 3). This relationship is comfortable and has very few ups and down. In some ways it is quite similar to the first style but with slightly more involvement. However, the involvement is not very exciting, and once routines and habits have been established, they vary little. A humdrum routine sets in and lasts for many years.

DIAGRAM 3

PASSIVE-CONGENIAL MARRIAGE

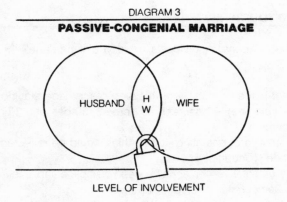

LEVEL OF INVOLVEMENT

WHAT DO YOU THINK?

1. What happens to individuals in this type of marriage?

2. What is the probability of this type of marriage staying together? (Circle one): 90 percent, 70 percent, 50 percent, 30 percent, 15 percent.

3. What style of parenting do you think would be reflected by this marriage? (Underline):
   a. Authoritative—balance between discipline and love
   b. Democratic—everyone has a say
   c. Indulgent—parents offer incentives for proper behavior
   d. Authoritarian—parents make the rules
   e. Neglectful—not much attention paid to children
   f. Instructor and guide—parent plays role of a teacher
   g. Permissive—children allowed to do their own thing

4. Describe the kind of family atmosphere you feel this marriage would create for the children.

5. What positive and negative qualities might appear in the children from this type of marriage?

Total Marriage

A fourth type of marriage is the *total marriage*. It is characterized by constant togetherness and mutual interest. Every experience of life is shared with each other, and little or nothing is conducted separately. The relationship is very intense because of the closeness, but it is also fragile. Any minor change or alteration can rock the boat.

Individual growth is limited because the relationship is everything, which creates a degree of smothering and stifling. Often this marriage is held out to be the ideal because "they are so close and do everything together!" In time, one or both may feel constricted and boxed-in because attempts to change on their part may be resisted.

Even when suggested changes are positive and beneficial, efforts are blocked. Any change upsets the precious and delicate equilibrium that has been established.

Another title for this marriage is the *eggshell relationship*. One false step and "crunch" goes the relationship. This marriage is depicted in Diagram 4.

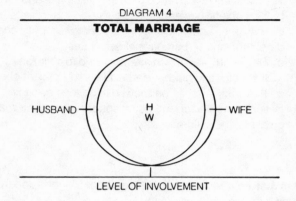

DIAGRAM 4

TOTAL MARRIAGE

HUSBAND — | H W | — WIFE

LEVEL OF INVOLVEMENT

WHAT DO YOU THINK?

1. What happens to individuals in this type of marriage?

2. What is the probability of this type of marriage staying together? (Circle one): 90 percent, 70 percent, 50 percent, 30 percent, 15 percent.

3. What style of parenting do you think would be reflected by this marriage? (Underline):
   a. Authoritative—balance between discipline and love
   b. Democratic—everyone has a say
   c. Indulgent—parents offer incentives for proper behavior
   d. Authoritarian—parents make the rules
   e. Neglectful—not much attention paid to children
   f. Instructor and guide—parent plays role of a teacher
   g. Permissive—children allowed to do their own thing

4. Describe the kind of family atmosphere you feel this marriage would create for the children.

5. What positive and negative qualities might appear in the children from this type of marriage?

Vital Marriage

A fifth type of marriage is the *vital marriage*. Each person is very involved in the other's interests, but they are not locked into the restrictions of the "total" marriage. In this marriage the couple likes to do things together whenever possible and, as much as possible, they share all roles within the marriage. They are not locked into stereotyped male and female roles. Thoughts and feelings are open to each other and communication is extensive between the two. The honesty that is so vital in building a marriage is present. Much of the marriage is together, but each has maintained his own individuality and uniqueness. Diagram 5 depicts this type of marriage.

DIAGRAM 5

VITAL MARRIAGE

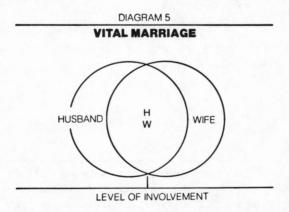

LEVEL OF INVOLVEMENT

Husband and wife cooperate in running the home, rearing the children, managing finances, and making decisions. They face and work through disagreements and the spouses are supportive to each other. This marriage usually contains reasonably well-adjusted people who are willing to take the risk of making changes to enhance and enrich their marriage.

WHAT DO YOU THINK?

1. What happens to individuals in this type of marriage?

2. What is the probability of this type of marriage staying together? (Circle one): 90 percent, 70 percent, 50 percent, 30 percent, 15 percent.

3. What style of parenting do you think would be reflected by this marriage (Underline):
    a. Authoritative—balance between discipline and love
    b. Democratic—everyone has a say
    c. Indulgent—parents offer incentives for proper behavior
    d. Authoritarian—parents make the rules
    e. Neglectful—not much attention paid to children
    f. Instructor and guide—parent plays role of a teacher
    g. Permissive—children allowed to do their own thing

4. Describe the kind of family atmosphere you feel this marriage would create for the children.

5. What positive and negative qualities might appear in the children from this type of marriage?

Troubled and struggling marriages do not make the task of parenting any easier. If the stability and cooperative teamwork needed in parenting is shaky and lacking in your marriage, before becoming parents, read the following books. Discuss and apply their contents in your marriage.

Communication: Key to Your Marriage by H. Norman Wright. Ventura, CA: Regal Books.

The Pillars of Marriage by H. Norman Wright. Ventura, CA: Regal Books.

Forty Ways to Say I Love You by James Bjorge. Minneapolis: Augsburg Publishing House.
What Wives Wish Their Husbands Knew About Women by Jim Dobson. Wheaton: Tyndale House Publishers.
You're Someone Special by Bruce Narramore, Grand Rapids: Zondervan Publishing House.

Potential Parenting Style

Now let's take a look at your potential parenting style. Most parents model many of the same parenting characteristics their parents modeled, whether they want to or not, because few couples take any steps to change their own attitudes about parenting or acquire new ideas and skills.

Many homes today (both Christian and non-Christian) are *closed*. This type of home exists in many forms and, because it is closed, does not always display its characteristics clearly. Suppression prevails in this home, and the children tend to be closed as well.

This atmosphere may be described as defensive, restrictive, protective, punitive, judgmental, fearful of change, blaming, possessive, and overly strict, with much emphasis on conformity. The family may be very concerned with status, reputation, and fixed roles. In this home atmosphere, it is difficult for a person's self-image to develop. It is difficult also for true nurturing as expressed in Ephesians 6:4 to occur. This home probably fails to fulfill Colossians 3:21: "Fathers, do not provoke or irritate or fret your children—do not be hard on them or harass them; lest they become discouraged and sullen and morose and feel inferior and frustrated; do not break their spirit"(*AMP*). This home is in violation of scriptural teaching for parenting.

Another type of home atmosphere is called *hang loose*. No guidance or direction is given; there are few rules or anything else that could give stability; concern for one another is often lacking. This home is often swayed or easily influenced by outside factors. In homes like this, children are rarely encouraged because the parents really don't care. Mom and Dad are interested only in themselves.

This home fails to give support and encouragement to the

children even when it is needed most. Often inconsistency is evident here—rules are enforced one day and not the next, which reflects a lack of strong values. Decisions in this home are made from a self-centered point of view.

A child needs a sounding board, but some parents do not allow themselves to be used as a sounding board. These parents are indifferent. A child feels very alone and lost because he doesn't have what is needed to develop his identity. With no interest directed toward him, he may not feel interest in himself. He doesn't know where he stands and thus becomes insecure. If he had a choice, he would rather be known as a "bad child" than a "nothing child."

Indifferent parents have a variety of parenting styles. One parent may see himself as permissive and feel good about it because he does not impose anything on the child. Other parents feel that even at an early age a child should be allowed to do his own thing and learn from his mistakes and take care of himself. These parents do not seem to care for their children. While freedom and responsibility should be granted gradually as a child increases in age and is capable developmentally of handling more, parents need to give direction in the early years.

Another style of parenting is the *dropout*. There are many kinds of dropouts. Some parents become overburdened by the strain of parenthood and give up. Some parents just don't like children. Some never wanted a child. Others become overwhelmed in the first few weeks after the child's birth. Some were caring parents initially and then changed. Some others cared nothing at all from the onset. This abandonment cannot help but create a sense of rejection within the child. Some abandonment occurs on an emotional level. Children are seen as a chore, and the resentment within the parent is transmitted to the child. Often this child develops into a parent who repeats the process. This style also violates Scripture, for the admonitions in Ephesians 6:4 and Proverbs 22:6 and numerous other passages are ignored.

Children have a right to expect certain things from their parents:

1. A father and mother who love each other and show it daily in small ways and big ways

2. Two persons who place on their list of priorities God first, then each other, and their children third

3. Two interested, kind, and loving guides; two examples—not perfect, but good

4. Parents who put relationships first, always (before rules, what others may think, etc.)

5. Enough time in the average week with parents (actually present, in person) to build a relationship. Regular times to talk (one-to-one)

6. To be allowed to be a child; the right to feel and think as an individual

7. Expressed affection, appreciation, and respect

8. The feeling of being understood; it is often difficult for parents to accept and understand why what is serious to them cannot be as serious to their children

9. Consistent, reinforcing acceptance; to be treated as a valuable, capable human being; never being torn down, never being attacked personally

10. To be listened to always (not unhearing anger or patient endurance until you can "tell them a thing or two")

11. Parents who never treat lightly what is important to a child

12. An attractive home—one of order and tranquility (most of the time, that is)

13. The right to privacy

14. Guidance in forming good health habits; (being overweight is more than just a physical burden to bear)

15. Information about God, the Bible, a relationship with Christ, life, worthy goals, values, standards, sex, morals, alcohol, and drugs

16. A single standard for both parents and the children regarding alcohol, drugs, honesty, church attendance, etc.[2]

Parents who have a healthy sense of self-esteem have a greater potential for a quality marriage and healthy parenting skills than those who don't. A common malady seen in a family with low parental self-esteem is perfectionism. A perfectionist is never satisfied with himself, his spouse, or his children. Many parents like this inhibit their positive emotions. They need to be in control constantly. Perfectionism is a type of rejection. Often overprotection is evident because the parents cannot trust either their children or themselves. Not trusting a child is evidence of not trusting the job one has been doing as a parent. With overprotectiveness in any atmosphere a person learns conformity but not responsibility, and deception is a common result.

The legalism that prevails in this atmosphere is a sign of parental personal insecurity. He or she lacks personal freedom and is quite constricted. The legalist often seeks a position in a school or church or other setting where others will support or reinforce his legalism.

In this home the double bind is often in operation. The double bind is a way of controlling by inducing guilt. It works as well in a marriage relationship as it does with children. Choices are given to others, but the choices are so structured that one is bound to feel guilty no matter what he or she does. "Go ahead and go with your friends and have a good time; I'll stay home and be happy mowing the lawn" is a common form.

WHAT DO YOU THINK?

1. Circle any of the following terms that describe the family atmosphere in which you were reared:

defensive	overly strict
protective	conforming
judgmental	few rules
restrictive	no concern for others
punitive	low self-esteem
fearful of change	overprotective
blaming	rigid
possessive	double bind

2. What were the positive characteristics of your home?

3. What were the positive characteristics of your spouse's home?

4. If you could have changed one thing about your family life as you were growing up, what would it have been?

5. What will you do to make sure this does not occur in your own family?

Nurturing and Enabling

Hopefully your family atmosphere will *not* reflect negative characteristics but will reflect the presence of Jesus Christ working in each person's life. A family atmosphere has the opportunity to reflect our position in Christ and who we really are because of Him (see 1 Pet. 2:9). You are a chosen possession. So is your spouse. So are your children.

We are also co-heirs with Christ because of His grace. This signifies an equality. Our behavior and attitude toward one another can reflect our relationship as joint or co-heirs.

Respect rather than degradation is to be the byword in our homes. This word means "to consider worthy of high regard." We look at our children in this way and perhaps in doing so we will encourage them to grow to their full potential rather than overly restricting them. Our home atmosphere can reflect an encouragement to grow. *Nurture* as used in Ephesians 6:4 is one form of growth and development. Another word is *enable*, which means to make possible or easy.

Enabling means that you take time to think, plan, and gather resources. This past summer Joyce and I were on vacation in the Grand Tetons by ourselves for a few days. For years I had dreamed of the time when she would be able to hike into a favorite back country lake with me and fish. So we planned for this. She exercised and so did I, but I still felt that the walk in and out on the same day might be too strenuous because of the distance and elevation. So I contacted a stable and secured the services of a guide and two horses. On a bright warm summer morning we met the guide, mounted the horses, and in less than two hours were on the shore of a beautiful lake. Four hours later, after catching and releasing (except for a few we took out to eat) 27 cutthroat trout, we headed up a steep trail to the mountain pass and down to the meadow four miles distant. I carried the poles, knapsacks, fish, and just about everything. Why? To enable Joyce to make the hike with ease. This was a delightful and tiring experience for both of us.

Enabling is a role that both father and mother can take to assist their child. When one parent enables and the other restricts, a child becomes torn. Agreement in style and manner of producing growth is also an ingredient. Consistent parents are usually stable and self-disciplined. Nonjudgmental listening can lead to a strong empathic relationship which fulfills the scriptural pattern of Galatians 6:1 and 1 Thessalonians 5:11.

Parents with a positive self-image are people who have the capacity to give and openly demonstrate love and affection, which are necessary to build a child's self-image. Throughout your years of parenthood your self-image may suffer from time to time. It will really fluctuate if it is based on your performance as a parent, at work, or in any other activity. Realizing that you are accepted and loved regardless of your performance is exciting. It frees you to perform as parents out of your sense of acceptance instead of striving as a parent to be accepted. We are accepted because of God's grace (see Eph. 2:8). The extent of our acceptance is evident in this description.[3]

God is very gracious to each of us. As our heavenly Father, He sets our parental pattern before us. Our example is seen in the definition of the word *gracious*. It means "accepting, kind, courteous, pleasing, and merciful." These are the qualities that a child must have in order to develop and mature.

"This, then, is the wonder of the Christian message, that God is this kind of God, that He loves me, and is not 'turned off' by my sins, my failures, my inadequacies, my insignificance. I am not a stranger in a terrifying universe. I am not a disease crawling on the face of an insignificant speck in the vast emptiness of space. I am not a nameless insect waiting to be crushed by an impersonal boot. I am not a miserable offender cowering under the glare of an angry deity. I am a man, beloved by God, Himself. I have touched the very heart of the universe and found His name to be Love. And that love has reached me, not because I have anything to boast about, but because of what He is, and because of what Christ has done for me in the Father's name. And I can believe this about God, and therefore, about myself, because Christ has come from the Father and is revealed by His teaching, by His life, by His death, by His very person that this is what God is like, He is full of grace.''[4]

WHAT'S YOUR PLAN?

1. What specific steps will you take to enrich your marriage during the next year?

2. Search through the Epistles and list 10 passages you would like to apply to your own life at the present time.

    (1)

    (2)

    (3)

    (4)

    (5)

    (6)

    (7)

    (8)

    (9)

   (10)

Notes

All material quoted is used by permission.
1. John F. Cuber and Peggy B. Haroff, ''The More Total View: Relationships Among Men and Women of the Upper Middle Class,'' *Marriage and Family Living*, vol. 25 (1963), pp. 140-145.
2. H. Norman Wright, *The Family That Listens* (Wheaton: Victor Books, 1978), pp. 50,51.
3. Adapted from H. Norman Wright, *Characteristics of a Caring Home* (Santa Ana, CA: Vision House, 1979), pp. 32,33.
4. Joseph Cooke, *Free for the Taking* (Old Tappan, NJ: Fleming H. Revell, 1975), pp. 29,30.

CHAPTER THREE/MARVIN N. INMON

Expectations and Myths of Parenthood

When children are young, they often "play house"—one child plays the father and another plays the mother, and if more than two are playing the others become the children. They quickly assume their roles, imitating the behaviors of their own parents. But children do not think much about their future roles as real parents. As these children proceed through the teenage years and embark upon adulthood they court, get engaged, marry, and—for most—become parents.

During this time of life, young adults have many expectations for forthcoming children and for themselves as parents. They have an idea about how many children they will have, what their sexes will be, when they will be born, what their personalities will be like, who they will look like, the vocations they will follow, and so on. Prospective parents also have an idea about how they will perform as parents—how they will teach their children, what kind of discipline they will use, how their schedules will be arranged, etc.

We all are motivated by expectations. When our expectations are fulfilled we are satisfied, When they are not fulfilled we are disappointed, sad, depressed, or even angry. Many of our expectations originated in our childhood. Looking back to your childhood will help you become aware of some of your expectations.

WHAT DO YOU THINK?

1. List five expectations you had regarding children when you married.

(1)

(2)

(3)

(4)

(5)

2. What are your current expectations concerning the following?

When will you have your (next) child?

What sex do you expect your child will be?

Where will the child be born?

Do you expect the father to be present for the birth?

Will the mother work after birth?

3. What are your spouse's expectations for the areas listed above? How do you know?

4. List 10 expectations you have for yourself as a parent and for your child.

    (1)

    (2)

    (3)

    (4)

    (5)

    (6)

    (7)

    (8)

    (9)

    (10)

5. Which of these expectations does your spouse have?

How Important Are Expectations?

How important are expectations and how do they affect us? A group of psychiatrists said this about expectations:

"Expectation involves such important aspects of personality as faith and hope—ingredients essential to human life. But hand in hand with expectation goes a certain amount of disappointment. The relationship between them affects the feelings that parents have about themselves and their children and influences how they act toward their children. Most of all, it determines how parents feel about having been parents as they look back in their later years.

"The expectations that people have about parenthood are as varied as are most things about human beings. Many of them are conscious. Most people, if asked what they expect parenthood to be, can say a good deal about it. At the same time, many are partially or completely unconscious and come out only in parents' attitudes and behavior. The unconscious expectations, because of their unrealistic elements (and there are always some of these), may take a long time to be modified by the way things really are. The more parents can unravel these unconscious expectations, the more they can fit their expectations and their actual life experiences together."[1]

Sometimes what we expect to happen and what in fact happens are very different. Listen to the experience of one couple whose expectations were fulfilled in quite a different way than they had expected.

In the first few years of our marriage we chose not to have children because I was busy as a youth pastor. Finally we decided, "Now is the time." After awhile, even though we were praying about it and doing everything we knew to do, we still had no children. We began to wonder why. Having children was one of our greatest expectations.

Both of us underwent a series of medical tests to find out about our potential for having children. The results indicated that we probably never could have children. At that same time God was definitely setting our directions toward further graduate training, so we settled in to graduate school and in the process tried to forget about those first test results.

A year later we underwent more tests. This time word came back to us very strongly from our doctor: "I think the best prospect for you would be to apply for adoption as soon as possible." As he explained the adoption process to us we began to accept that we would have no children of our own. Then, as we got hold of ourselves and hold of the Lord's love for us, we began to work through the adoption process.

We were told by the state agency that it would take four to five years to go through the process of adopting a newborn child. We wondered about God's purpose in all of this, but we applied and were put on the waiting list.

Again we were discouraged, this time because there were several hundred people ahead of us on the waiting list, so we reconsidered our goals. We decided we would be willing to take an older child for adoption—one of our race, one who might be emotionally handicapped if it could be corrected with love, even one with a physical handicap. This time we were told that even adopting an older child could take two to three years. We waited.

About a year later while we were at a wedding in another state, we talked with a friend who had been a youth sponsor in the church I had served as youth pastor. My wife shared with her heart-to-heart about our desires for a child, and our friend brought some special words of comfort when she said, "I don't think God would give you such an intense desire if He were not going to honor it down the road." She said, "I'm going to push you guys right to the top of my prayer list, and I'm going to pray that God will either diminish your desire for a newborn or work out the details."

Shortly after we returned home, we received a call from a friend who asked how our adoption plans were coming. We answered that there had been no change since we talked to him about three weeks ago. And he said, "I know of a potential for a child." He didn't have very much information except that a young woman who was pregnant had decided to give up her child for adoption. We asked him some questions—such as when is the baby due? I had several months left in school. My wife had planned to continue working until October and I was involved in the process of beginning a new ministry. So much was going on that even though we were planning to adopt, we really wondered if this was the best time.

Our friend called back on Saturday night and told us, "She's due in four weeks." Our first response was, "Only four weeks!" Everyone else we know had nine months to get ready for the occasion. It really startled us.

He put us in touch with social workers and a lawyer in his state, and we contacted social workers and a lawyer in our state to begin the process of a private adoption. The interstate adoption laws are tough, so in the process we really had to continue committing things to the Lord.

As a result, a remarkable thing happened. The girl who was having the baby accepted the Lord. She felt that God was very specifically telling her to give her child up for adoption and she wanted to talk to us. We called our lawyer in that state and called our lawyer in our state and they arranged for us to talk with her because she had a series of questions she wanted to ask to find out if we were the ones who should have the child. She felt led not only to ask us the questions but also to write down the answers beforehand that she wanted to hear. We had no knowledge of this when we started an hour-and-a-half telephone conversation with her—probably the heaviest conversation of my life. At the end of that conversation she very sweetly and simply thanked the Lord right there over the phone. She said, "I do believe that you are to be the parents of the child I am carrying." We had a couple other brief conversations with her by telephone, and then we waited.

I was working one day in our apartment at the seminary when a good friend came bursting in. As he came through the door he hollered, "She's in labor." He had received the call because I had taken our phone off the hook so I wouldn't be disturbed. Because the child was to be born in a natural childbirth clinic where, if all goes well, the mother and child go home within two or three hours after the birth, we had given the phone numbers of several friends in case we could not be reached.

The delivery was not expected until midnight, so we waited until my wife arrived home from her nursing shift. When we got on the plane, I felt numb because I knew that in a few hours our joy and one little gal's loss would be tremendous. We were picked up by friends at the airport and went to their home. When we arrived, we received word that the delivery was expected earlier—within the hour.

We jumped in the car and drove to the natural childbirth clinic. About 10 minutes later, down the corridor came a little cry, and the doctor brought our little daughter to us.

As we drove back to our friends' home, we were full of the joy of the Lord because we had given one of our highest expectations to Him—even after some struggles—and He had given back to us more delight and more joy than we ever thought possible.

WHAT DO YOU THINK?

1. If you were the couple in this situation, how would you have responded to the medical test results, the adoption process, and the sudden news that a child was to be born and needed a home?

2. How would your spouse have responded?

3. In what ways could you adjust your expectations? List five adjustments you would be willing to make.

(1)

(2)

(3)

(4)

(5)

4. Are there any circumstances you fear may occur? Does your spouse know of your fear? Share any fears after you have written them here.

Some Common Expectations

All parents-to-be have expectations about the pregnancy, the birth, how well the infant will sleep through the night, and how soon he will crawl, walk, and talk. These expectations are natural for they originate from our past experiences in our own families and with other families. We must realize, however, that there are differences from individual to individual on the progress of pregnancy, birth, amount of sleep, and age at which the infant accomplishes the feats of crawling, walking, and talking.

Beyond the expectations for physical and mental development are expectations for personality development. A common expectation among parents is that their child will have the same values and beliefs as they have. Parents want to see their own lives carried on in the life of their child. If the child develops different values and beliefs, the parents may have trouble letting go of their child, and too great an attachment creates stress for the parents.

Another common expectation is that the child will achieve in the areas in which the parents feel deficient. The parents may want and even demand that the child make up for what they feel is lacking in their own lives.

"Some expectations may be largely fulfilled, may work out the way the parents hoped, and disappointment kept to a minimum. More often, especially if the expectations mean a great deal, the reality falls short in some way, and parents have to cope with definite disappointment. Here the wound may be double. If children fall short in areas where the parents are satisfied with themselves, at least the self-satisfaction remains; but if the child fails to make up for an earlier frustration, it is a second blow to the parents. The danger of this kind of double disappointment is that acceptance of the children on their own terms is then extremely difficult."[2]

A child needs to be accepted as he is and allowed to develop as a unique person. Of course parents should instill biblical values in their child, but beyond that they must allow room for differences in likes and dislikes.

WHAT DO YOU THINK?

How can prospective or new parents adjust to or clarify their expectations? Here is a step-by-step procedure:

1. Carefully think through and list all of your expectations and discuss them together as a couple.

2. Determine the origin of these expectations and why they are important.

3. For each of your expectations, describe what will happen if that expectation is not met.

4. In place of expectations, develop some specific goals for yourselves as parents and for your child's development.

Other People's Expectations

Not only do you have expectations of yourself and your child, but others also have expectations of you and your child as well. Who are these people? Friends and grandparents!

Some in-laws look forward to becoming grandparents and have their own way of pressuring a couple to "produce." Other grandparents resent being grandparents.

Sometimes if the child does not look like the grandparents, is not the sex they were hoping for, or does not behave according to their expectations, grandparents display their disappointment.

Frequently parents complain about how grandparents treat the grandchildren when they come for a visit. Some grandparents say, "When my grandchild is in my home, I'll treat him the way I want to. If I want to spoil the child, that's my privilege." Naturally, such an attitude can create dissension between families.

What if the grandchildren prefer one set of grandparents over the other and want to spend time with their favorite and not with the other? These difficulties are really quite common.

Here is a list of questions for you and your spouse to discuss and then, if you are brave, to discuss with the grandparents.

WHAT DO YOU THINK?

1. Do the grandparents want a boy or a girl grandchild?

2. Are they hoping to have the child named after them?

3. Which grandmother expects to help out at the time of birth? What if they both live close?

4. What type of assistance around the house are they expecting from the new father during the first few weeks?

5. What suggestions will they make (or have they made) for rearing the child? How will you respond to these?

6. How will you respond if one of them says, "You're doing it all wrong"?

7. How will you convey to another family member that he is handling or feeding (or whatever) the child differently than you do and that you prefer him to do it your way?

8. In what areas would you like some assistance from the grandparents?

9. Do the grandparents expect you to use your vacations to visit them with their grandchild? What do you plan to do?

10. Have you asked your parents and in-laws what they do expect from you and the child? What expectations do they have for being involved in the baby's life?

In regard to grandparents, Robert H. Hall said, "As for prospective grandmothers, it is difficult to convince some of them that their role has become a passive one and it is impossible to convince others that they should play any role at all. Rare is the pregnant woman's mother who knows when to come in and when to stay out of the picture. But now is the time for you to try to define your mother's role in your life if you haven't already and if you ever hope to."[3]

Expectations and Goals
Expectations have different characteristics from goals. Expec-

tations involve looking forward to something with a degree of certainty that it will occur. Expectations contain assumptions often without any effort, direction, or valid reason for their existence.

Many parents are frustrated because they fail to find in themselves or in their child what they expected to find, and they are troubled because they did not expect something they eventually encounter. As prospective parents you should begin to set some goals for what you desire in yourselves and also set some goals for some positive character traits you would like to see develop in your child according to his abilities and potentials. There must be a sense of acceptance for the uniqueness of the child *and* flexibility in the goals that are set for him and eventually with him. "It is pleasant to see plans develop. That is why fools refuse to give them up even when they are wrong" (Prov. 13:19, *TLB*).

A goal is different from an expectation, for it is a statement involving faith (which is, according to Heb. 11:1, "the substance of things hoped for, the evidence of things not seen," *KJV*). It tells of something we hope will happen in the future. Involved in goals is the process of establishing specific plans and steps to attain the goals.

WHAT DO YOU THINK?

1. List five specific goals you have for yourself as a parent.
   (1)

   (2)

   (3)

   (4)

   (5)

2. What can you do to attain these goals?

3. List five goals you have for your child. Remember that you will probably have to alter these goals later depending on the child's uniqueness.

(1)

(2)

(3)

(4)

(5)

4. What can you do to assist your child to attain these goals?

5. Describe how your goals are different from expectations.

A Personal Experience

I, too, have struggled through expectations and goals. Let me take you back when my daughter Nancy was very young. I remember one evening, or I should say early morning, when I rolled over and stared at the lighted dial on the digital clock. Ominously it read 3:00. That is 3:00 A.M. It had only been two hours since the last time that soft cry across the hall had summoned us. Soft, yes, yet so demanding of attention.

That scene would be repeated many times during the next several weeks. Our daughter would cry for either her mother or me to respond to her needs. My wife Rita and I had decided to be different from other Christian parents we had observed in our church and in our personal relationships. We wanted our child to adjust to *our* life-style, especially since we were so comfortable with it. Having been married for 12 years before the birth of our first child did pose special problems for us as parents. Those who have children know that it is easy to say that a child should adjust to their parents' schedule. It is a very different thing to learn that it does not work that way.

While adjusting to the birth of a child poses a number of problems for new parents, we must remember that Scripture identifies a child as a gift of the Lord and a reward (see Ps. 127:3). James says that "every good thing bestowed and every perfect gift is from above" (Jas. 1:17), and that means that little one sleeping—or crying—across the hall is truly a gift from God. In times of adjustments, these become the watchwords of Christian parenthood.

Time is probably the greatest adjustment Rita and I have had to make. Since Nancy's birth, it seems there is not enough time for anything except her. Our very regulated household, which had run on a regimented schedule, was suddenly plunged into complete chaos. Our entire world was focused around the needs of this new arrival. This situation forced us to spend most of our waking hours and much of our sleeping time meeting them. Her needs included filling a bottomless stomach, trying to dry up the fountain, keeping one step ahead of the dirty laundry, and being a parent whose only lot in life is being seasick from spending bedless hours in the rocking chair.

Because "there is a time for every event under heaven" (Eccl. 3:1), God must have had some reason for creating a child with such dependence on her parents. Actually, the time demands are God's way of showing us how marvelous His gift is. This is the lesson God is teaching Rita and me. If Nancy were able to take care of herself we would not see her grow into the child and woman that

God would have her become. It is very possible that the relationship we are endeavoring to build could be torn down by a lack of involvement or attentiveness if we took for granted that Nancy would survive.

Looking at Ecclesiastes 3, we noticed that God tells us that we are to see good in all our labor, as it is a gift from God, and that there is nothing better for us than to rejoice and do good in our lifetime. The most difficult periods of adjustment for Rita and me come when we do not see Nancy as a gift, but when we see her as labor, toil, and a drudgery to be endured rather than enjoyed. It is at those times that we have a tendency to feel alienated from our daughter and from each other.

Again looking at Ecclesiastes 3 and the appointed time for everything, the process of alienation comes when our thought lives are focused on the negative aspects of our relationship with Nancy. When we look at our daughter through our frustration, it is easy to be reminded of the negative aspects of the passage:

- of a time to tear down
- of a time to weep
- of a time to mourn
- of a time to throw stones
- of a time to shun embracing
- of a time to give up as lost
- of a time to throw away
- of a time to tear apart
- of a time to be silent
- of a time to hate
- of a time to war
- of a time to uproot what has been planted
- and a time for a relationship to die.

It is easy to ask in a time like this what profit there is to the worker (or parent) from that in which he toils. When we are reminded that the three of us labored together in a hospital when the appointed time was "a time to give birth," we draw closer to one another and adjust to one another.

Our joy is more complete when we think on the positive aspects of Nancy's arrival and growth:

- that she came from a time to plant

- that she is a gift and a time to heal
- it is our time to build up
- a time to laugh
- a time to dance
- a time to embrace
- a time to search
- a time to keep
- a time to sew together
- a time to speak
- a time to love
- and a time for peace.

The key to our adjusting to Nancy rests in the goals and priorities that we have established for our lives. The purpose to which God has called us is that we give glory to God. It is our hope and prayer that all we do is consistent with that purpose (see Hab. 2:14).

One of the life goals that we have established for ourselves and our home is that we invest our lives in others. Nancy is one of the others with whom we have become involved. One of the ways that we can invest our lives in her is through the meeting of her day-to-day needs. By knowing that she is fed, warm, dry, and happy, we know that we have been able to contribute to her growth.

A potential danger to the husband-wife relationship is the placement of the child in a position of higher priority than that of the spouse. Early in our married life Rita and I established some priorities, which we have tried to keep, regarding the several ministries to which we have been called. The most important ministry that God has given to me is Rita herself. Keeping our priorities straight has allowed me also to keep these relationships and ministries in perspective.

In my counseling ministry I find that my clients change regularly. In my teaching ministry students come and go. In the church ministry parishioners change. Even my daughter will eventually grow up and leave home. Therefore, Rita is the only ministry that God has given me for a lifetime. It is my opinion that if I fail in this lifetime ministry, then I have failed in the ministry.

Rita communicates this same priority of ministry to me. The priorities that Rita and I have established for ourselves are these:

1. Our relationship with the Lord
2. Our relationship with each other
3. Our relationship with our daughter
4. Our relationship with our ministries.

Because we have placed each other ahead of our daughter and are able to keep and review our priorities regularly, the adjustment process of adding a child to our family has been greatly eased.

We challenge you to set goals for your lives and to establish working priorities. These give you a road map by which you can truly see God's plan for your lives together.

WHAT'S YOUR PLAN?

1. What reactions do you have to this personal experience? Why?

2. List five feelings you experienced in reading this story.
   (1)
   (2)
   (3)
   (4)
   (5)

3. What specifically can you do this week that will apply the contents of this chapter to your life?

Notes

All material quoted is used by permission.
1. Committee on Public Education, Group for the Advancement of Psychiatry, *The Joys and Sorrows of Parenthood* (New York: Charles Scribner's Sons, 1973), pp. 31,32.
2. *Ibid.*, pp. 34,35.
3. Robert E. Hall, *Nine Months' Reading: A Medical Guide for Pregnant Women* (New York: Doubleday & Company, Inc., 1960), p. 56.

What Is a Mother?

The word *mother* is very subjective and has different meanings for different people. To some it sounds so old, so responsible, so confirming, so permanent and final. Some think of "good mothers"; some think of "bad mothers." The word evokes memories of kindness, understanding, hard work, self-sacrifice, and love; or it evokes memories of nagging, laziness, narrow-mindedness, selfishness, and distrust. As we think about these words, it is hard to imagine a mother deliberately choosing to exhibit the negative characteristics, yet some do. By preparing for motherhood, you can choose the positive characteristics.

There are many examples of mothers in the Bible. More than 100 mothers are mentioned in the Old Testament and 18 in the New.

In the Old Testament books of Kings and Chronicles, greater stress is laid on the character of the mothers than the fathers. Some were righteous, and some were described as wicked, such as Athaliah. "For the sons of the wicked Athaliah had broken into the house of God and even used the holy things of the house of the Lord for the Baals" (2 Chron. 24:7).

Isaiah gave a eulogy to a mother's spiritual role when he drew the analogy of one "whom his mother comforteth, so will I comfort you" (66:13, *KJV*). He conveyed the certainty and degree of divine love and compared it to the highest example of love at the human level—a mother's love for her child. David paid tribute to motherhood when he described deepest grief as that of "one that mourneth for his mother" (Ps. 35:14, *KJV*). This grief is illustrated in Isaac's grief at the death of his mother, Sarah.

Deborah's highest title was "a mother in Israel" (Judg. 5:7). Hannah was a symbol of motherly love (see 1 Sam. 2). She was often referred to as the prayerful mother and greatly influenced Samuel's entire life.

Another mother from Tekoah (see 2 Sam. 14:1-20) was noted for three distinct qualities: eloquence, tact, and wisdom.

In the New Testament, several mothers were noted. Elizabeth, the mother of John the Baptist, and Mary, the mother of Jesus, are two who come to mind. Timothy's mother Eunice was noted for her life of faith.

WHAT DO YOU THINK?

(Wife) What would you like to be noted for as a mother?

(Husband) What would you like your wife to be noted for as a mother?

Motherhood and a Career

With a baby come some changes in life-style. If a woman has been employed or involved in a career what happens when a baby is on the way? Does a baby interfere with a career? Where does a mother's responsibility rest—at home with the child or pursuing the career? Practically speaking, a child does interfere with careers of working parents.

Opinions vary about combining a career with motherhood. Each of these roles will face some limitations and loss of flexibility and freedom. If a career is primary, it appears that a child is "crowded in" to the existing schedule. More and more mothers today are choosing to have both. But at the same time others are adhering strongly to the idea that they are not about to have a child for somebody to raise.

If a career woman defers returning to her job for several years, when she does resume her career, her skills may be outdated and she may find herself at the bottom of the pay scale.

So what is best? What are the advantages and disadvantages of each alternative? What do others believe?

In 1972 and 1977, *Better Homes and Gardens* asked its readers how they felt about mothers having a career and related issues.

"Eighty-four percent of the respondents feel parents have the greatest influence on the general development of children under age 12. In answer to a somewhat different question in 1972, 74 percent said that parents have a greater effect than do influences outside the home. Television is named by 1977 respondents as the second greatest influence on children under 12 (48 percent), followed by friends (40 percent).

"Respondents generally feel it is important that the mother remain home while the children are young. A large majority (88 percent) say the mother should be home while the children are preschool age; 56 percent follow this through to grade school; 36 percent to junior high school; and 24 percent to high school.

"Seventy-two percent of the respondents think most working mothers do not spend enough time with their children. Eighty-six percent say this about the majority of fathers."[1]

Similar questions were asked in the 1979 Christian Marriage and Family Life Survey.[2] How would you respond to these questions?

WHAT DO YOU THINK?

1. There are more married women—with children—in the work force than ever before. Do you think this has had a harmful effect on family life? Why or why not?

2. Would you approve if the wife were the main breadwinner and the husband took responsibility for the house and children? Why or why not?

3. Which of the following do you think has the greatest influence on the general development of children under age 12? (Number from greatest [1] to least [10].)

_____ Friends
_____ Organized activities (sports, etc.)
_____ Television
_____ Books
_____ Teachers
_____ Church
_____ Parents
_____ Brothers and sisters
_____ Other relatives
_____ Other

4. At which point is it no longer necessary for the mother to remain at home? (Underline):

   a. Shortly after birth
   b. When the youngest child enters preschool
   c. When the youngest child enters grade school
   d. When the youngest child enters junior high school
   e. When the youngest child enters high school
   f. When the youngest child enters college
   g. Mother should always remain at home.

Turn to the end of this chapter to compare your answers with those of the 8,500 participants of this survey.

The Influence of Mother

A child is receptive to input immediately. Within the first 24 hours infants are capable of learning. Newborns have a very highly attuned capacity to receive new information through all senses. From birth on, the child benefits from sensory input, and even though he cannot understand it at this point he will learn to adjust himself to a higher level of stimulation. The child will learn to respond to a certain voice or physical characteristic of a parent.

When a baby is in the care of his own mother, an attitude is conveyed to the child that nobody else can convey. Mother-child attachment is quite important at this early stage of development.

A mother has a natural tendency to respond to her baby which stimulates him to respond. If a child-care worker, maid, or nurse is hired to do this task, it becomes a paid routine. The feelings, sensitivity, and depth of response that will be offered to a baby by a substitute mother are not the same. Those hired to care for a child may be unqualified to handle some of the problems that occur.

"It is risky to turn an infant in this critical early period of life over to someone who is unequipped to understand or respond to his real needs. He may learn patterns of behavior that cannot prove adaptive to your way of life. And he may find it difficult to learn certain kinds of behavior later on, having missed the periods when he normally would have done so.

"In the first weeks and months of life, the point is that the person who cares for the child, being more detached and 'objective' than his mother, may by this very token lack her sensitivity to his cues and tend to care for him by preconceived rules and convenient schedules rather than by responding to his own signals of need and signs of comfort. The important thing becomes keeping him clean, or getting him to finish his bottle and go off to sleep 'on time.' Under these circumstances a baby may receive adequate physical care and yet miss out on the amount of stimulation—the holding, handling and cuddling, the responsive faces, voices and hands—that give him an extra sense of pleasure in life beyond just being full and dry and that make other people seem worth relating to."[3]

Many mothers today are employed for numerous reasons. Here is Marvin and Rita Inman's personal experience:

After Nancy arrived, most of our friends assumed that Rita's career of 14 years was over. But it wasn't. Three months later Rita was back at work for one more year. This was not a snap decision but one that grew out of careful deliberation, communication and prayer. For one thing, this decision was an act of good stewardship of time and finances. Rita had one year remaining before the 15 year mark. This would bring more security benefits and a retirement income. And as we hoped for a second child soon the insurance benefits from her hospitalization plan needed to be considered; they were excellent and could not be duplicated elsewhere. I was just establishing myself in a new occupation after four years of graduate school. We had purchased a home and involved ourselves in our community. We needed both incomes at this time until my counseling practice expanded sufficiently to provide all we needed.

Our own personal choice entered into this decision as well. One of Rita's goals for several years had been to obtain the 15-year mark in her company. And because of her personal desire for this goal I was behind her 100 percent and willing to help out even more around home to make this a possibility.

When my wife and I made the decision that she would return to work after the birth of our first child, the first question to confront us was, Who would look after our daughter? Our search began with many phone calls to numerous advertisements and to recommendations of well-meaning friends.

The next day when I returned home expecting to find our child-care problem settled, it became obvious that something was definitely wrong! One look at my wife's face said that desperation was the mood for the evening. She had called more than 20 sitters, making some surprising and frustrating discoveries at each response. A sampling included the following:

"I don't do diapers."

"I don't take children under two."

"Bring the kid over, I'll see if it's calm enough."

"It's $50, $40, $30, $35 per week (in advance), you provide the food."

"I only use disposables."

"You pay even if the child is not here."

Some of the people had sounded too old, some too young, some incoherent or even unintelligible.

At this point my wife sat down and cried. "I can't leave our daughter in the hands of people like this. They seem more interested in the money than caring for a child."

"What are we going to do?" I asked.

I became upset thinking of what my wife went through that day. Were they all like this or were there any possibilities that sounded promising? There were four or five in this group that seemed to have some potential. Then came the most important statement my wife made that day. "What difference does it make? I don't know what I'm looking for and I don't know what you expect!"

Ouch. She was right again. Who were we going to entrust our daughter to, for up to eight hours a day, for the next year or more? We decided to sit down and put our expectations on paper, making a list of questions which we had in our minds about the person and services we were hiring. A very nonproductive day raised a number of questions which we felt were important. We needed these answered before we would be satisfied.

1. What do you charge?
2. What do you expect from us?
3. Are you licensed?
4. How many other children do you sit? What are their ages?
5. What activities are available for the children?
6. How much TV are the children allowed to watch?
7. Is food provided? What kind and how is it prepared?
8. Do you provide diapers?
9. What is your philosophy of child rearing?
10. Do you have children of your own?
11. If so, may we meet them?
12. What happens in an emergency?
13. What if you are sick or not available?
14. What is the extent of interaction with each child?
15. What do you do about our vacations? Do you take vacations?
16. What method of discipline do you use?
17. What provisions are there for first aid?
18. Do you have references?

Armed with our questions and a list of appointments, we embarked several days later feeling much better about the prospects of finding a competent sitter for our daughter.

The first three houses we pulled up to reminded us of historical monuments (the battle of Gettysburg, or "after the burning of Savannah"). We quickly crossed them off our list and moved on down the road. One very neat home contained an elderly couple. The husband was recovering from open-heart surgery and the wife smoked up a storm the entire time we were there. The children were completely ignored, being allowed to do as they pleased.

After several interviews we were becoming very discouraged and wondered if it might not be better to give up the idea of Rita's returning to work.

Fortunately, my wife had been saving the best for last. We pulled up to a neat home and were greeted graciously by a very happy woman. She immediately snatched up our daughter and began to develop rapport. As we went through each question, we became more pleased. When we found we were the first non-referral in two years, we were ecstatic. We also learned that our new sitter was a registered nurse who wanted to spend more time at home with her own daughter who was slightly retarded. Here we found what we had been praying for: someone whom we could trust, who loved children, who had experience, and who communicated well with both us and our daughter. Charlotte has been a dream come true and she is more than we could ever have hoped for.

It is still each couple's decision whether to combine a career and mothering. Many feel that a child has the greatest potential with the natural mother. But with the severe economic conditions that couples face, the pressure for both to be working is high. In order to provide more stability when mother must work, many couples are moving to a greater level of equal parenting involvement or adapting time schedules. This too is the type of decision that should be discussed in depth and taken before the Lord in prayer for His will in the matter.

Physical Transition

When a woman becomes a mother she enters a new phase of life. She also relinquishes a phase. In the process she will experience physical, emotional, and social transitions.

Pregnancy and childbirth may be the hardest work a woman's

body ever does. A woman needs to be prepared to look and feel different during pregnancy and following the birth of the child. If a woman cares for herself properly, she may feel and look better than before.

Pregnancy is a bit like moving into adolescence. In adolescence a girl is no longer a child but is not yet a woman. Feelings of anxiety, self-consciousness, and awkwardness abound. At times she likes what is occurring and on other occasions she would like to pull the stop switch. Pregnancy is a similar state—it is a state of becoming. On the developmental spectrum, a girl has moved to womanhood, and now a woman is adding motherhood. A new identity is being added.

This turning point is described by Anfela Barron McBride in her book, *The Growth and Development of Mothers*. "Your notion of bodily integrity is violated in a much more dramatic fashion than the advent of the first menses or the first act of intercourse. Even if you are not susceptible to the usual discomforts of pregnancy (ankle swelling, sore breasts, nausea, vomiting, fatigue, heartburn, feeling bloated, forgetting where you begin and end), you are bound to feel at times that your body has been possessed and that you have lost control of your own person. You can view it as a violent siege, and opportunity for physical transcendence, a chance to see if your body functions properly, or a slight inconvenience—well worth the price—but pleasure and pain will always go hand in hand, and ambivalence is the only correct, the only possible emotional posture. Every transition brings its share of fears (real dangers and specific problems) and anxieties (a diffuse sense of danger, unspecific tension), and they are in abundance when you are having a baby, which calls for a whole new life style."[4]

Elizabeth Hambrick-Stowe beautifully tells her experience of pregnancy in her book *Expecting:*

"Some of the questions that crossed my mind were minor. Would I be left with varicose veins? A bulging abdomen? Others were more thought-provoking. A life insurance company would not issue a policy on me after my sixth month of pregnancy. This took us—and our agent, who was ecstatic after more than a year of salesmanship to have finally written the policy!—completely by surprise. Regardless of how healthy the obstetrician might declare me, despite the complete medical supervision that far surpassed the company's knowledge of my husband who had not been to a doctor in four years—nevertheless, I was a bad risk. Childbirth was near, and I might die. In the light of this, I inquired about maternal mortality rates. The physician whom I asked never answered. Why, he queried, was I thinking such morbid thoughts?

"There were other serious questions that inevitably come to mind: Down's syndrome for example, and whether the baby was developing normally. I joined a local book discussion group one evening; our topic was the real-life story about a hemophiliac child and what his parents' and their family's lives were like with that disease. The child's disease had come upon them totally by surprise. . . . To none of these questions, major or minor, would I get an answer until the process of pregnancy was completed.

"In this passivity, in the midst of and because of what is happening within, unseen, and unknown—there comes the gift of grace.

"Grace is a beautiful word. It has a light touch upon the heart. Grace is a lifting release. In the human-holy partnership of pregnancy, grace means relaxation and trust. The hymn puts it in these words: 'Twas grace that taught my heart to fear, and grace my fears relieved.' In other words, you know exactly where you stand! There is comfort in that.

"Pregnancy gives a woman that kind of realism. There is a life developing within her. It is not her life; it lives off her. Sometimes it causes discomfort—nausea, low energy, loss of appetite, leg and back pains. Awkwardness and inconvenience are no strangers. There are periods when the pregnant woman needs the bathroom facilities constantly. Sleeping can be difficult. A habit that one never even thinks about—crossing the legs when sitting—must suddenly be avoided, as it puts additional strain on the blood circulation. Settled comfortably, warmly in bed, how many times I would suddenly remember and groan, 'The vitamins!' Up I would rise—quickly, in order not to give myself time to skip them 'just tonight'— to keep on the schedule of nutritional supplements.

"No, the mother does not know with what effects pregnancy will leave her. Nor does she know what the baby's life will do to her own life, particularly if it should be unhealthy or retarded in some way. It is not that one is unwilling to take these things on, but there are just so many unknowns. The nine months' timetable will not be hurried or delayed. *But that's all right.* For there is something larger, something greater, encompassing both her and her pregnancy.

In giving herself to the re-creation of life, the Christian receives grace—the grace of trust, the grace of sensing clearly that foundation of God that undergirds all our fragile existence. Touching on that bedrock, a pregnancy's grace is a gain far outweighing the surrender of seemingly autonomous control. Receiving this lifting release, the Christian in receiving partnership understands where lies true freedom from the blind powers surrounding and impacting human existence.''[5]

Emotional Transition

The emotional transition is closely tied to the physical changes. The bodily fatigue may counter the new joy and elation over being a mother.

''And the interrelationship goes even further: If your muscles are tense, you may become easily upset; if you do not eat food that nourishes you, life will be more difficult and less interesting. Your body is inactive, it may have a depressing effect on your thoughts. The condition of your body—how it feels and how you feel about it—can create confidence and self-esteem or the reverse, insecurity and depression.''[6]

As a woman moves along the path toward womanhood, she must accept absentmindedness as a common occurrence that intensifies as pregnancy continues. She must also accept her dreams; they will be vivid and intense and usually increase. They may seem real, but they are not. She should talk them over with her husband. In a common apprehensive dream the mother is mistreating her baby or not caring for it at all. This is only a legitimate fear, since she is just beginning to learn about motherhood. This is a time to dwell upon and apply Philippians 4:4,6: ''Rejoice in the Lord always—delight, gladden yourselves in Him; again I say, Rejoice! Do not fret or have any anxiety about anything, but in every circumstance and in everything by prayer and petition [definite requests] with thanksgiving continue to make your wants known to God'' *(AMP)*.

A mother-to-be may also have dreams of losing the baby. Dreams and nightmares about the baby dying are common. It is natural to be concerned about a baby's health. Dreams can be a vehicle of expressing fears and worries as well as hostilities toward the child. Some of these feelings may be unacceptable to bring to consciousness, so her dream becomes the avenue of expression. Remember that these are just dreams and if they help her get in touch with her feelings, they are helpful.

Fears of one kind or another occur during pregnancy. Acknowledge them. Tne mother-to-be needs to talk them over with others and discover the cause for these feelings. A husband's support is greatly needed at this time. It assures the wife that she will not be alone in the task of parenting. The husband may need some assurance and building up as well. Therefore, other significant people will need to assist.

Among the emotions a new mother will experience are rage, envy, anger, guilt, confusion, jealousy, self-love, and self-hate. The question is not, "Will I experience these emotions," but, "How will I handle them?" Negative emotions are simply telling you something about yourself.

WHAT DO YOU THINK?

How do you think a mother would respond to a child if she feels
Inadequate:
Competitive:

Resentful:

Judgmental:

Blame:

It is common to overcompensate, to be extra passive. overly kind and solicitous, and to judge and blame others.

Along with physical and emotional transitions there may be social isolation. The early months when the child is so dependent on its mother can bring feelings of confinement, isolation, and loneliness. A woman may experience these feelings especially if she was employed before becoming a mother. Performing a new role as mother, her husband gone much of the time, and no relatives close at hand all can lend themselves to isolation.

Maternal Myths
Beware of maternal myths that contribute to the emotional and social transitions. The "maternal instinct" myth states that all women have a built-in biological drive to have children and love them instantly and to know how to care for them. Remember that mothering must be learned, and even the desire to become a mother may need to be developed and nurtured. Motherly love in many cases is absent at first and needs to be developed. When these feelings or attitudes are not present initially, most mothers are afraid to share their concerns with anyone else, and thus guilt intensifies.

A woman needs to develop an identity for herself that is separate from that of her own mother. Developing her own identity may involve some struggle and guilt. She needs to accept the abilities and qualities in her own mother that she respected and valued and reject the ones she disagreed with. If she doesn't, she will tend to repeat what happened to her whether she liked all of it or not.

Some other myths of womanhood that abound are the following:

- A happy, fulfilled woman is a pregnant woman.
- A woman is still a girl until pregnant.
- When a woman feels incomplete and frustrated, the solution is to have a baby.
- Having a baby is the best way to please a husband.
- If you are having difficulties in your marriage, having a baby will help.
- A woman is grateful to her husband for making her pregnant.
- Since women were created capable of bearing children, they are lacking until they have a baby.

WHAT'S YOUR PLAN?

1. What do you think are other concerns a woman might have at this time?

2. What is the greatest fear in your own life about mothering (or, for husbands, about your wife mothering)? How can you deal with it?

3. (For the mother) What change in your life because of pregnancy do you fear will not change back after the baby is born?

(For the father) What change in your wife because of pregnancy do you fear will not change back after the baby is born?

4. What can be done at this time to insure greater confidence in becoming a mother?

When a woman is pregnant she is more sensitive to outside stresses. Any type of problem can be more difficult. Stress—whether it be health, marriage, in-laws, finances, or work—may hit harder and recovery may be slower. How a woman handles stress has an effect upon the fetus. If the stress lasts and lasts, fetal activity can increase significantly. Some studies indicate that a relationship may exist between emotional stress during pregnancy and overall restlessness in the baby. There could be a correlation between a mother's anxiety and a baby who cries more. If a mother is under stress, it could delay the natural bonding process which occurs at birth.[7]

The loss that occurs from the mother's perspective at this time adds to the stress. The apparent loss of freedom is one of the fears that many women have. There is a loss of freedom when it comes to spontaneity, schedule, neatness of the home, etc. All of this can be called a loss of movement. Mothers seem to be divided into two categories—those who resist, fight, and resent this loss of movement, and those who anticipate, accept, and plan for this loss or change. It is possible to determine in one's mind what she is willing and not willing to change. This can mean that the baby will not be blamed for taking away her freedom.

Another loss can be measured by a woman's comments about herself: "Boy, am I getting fat!" "I feel like a blimp, ugh." "I don't walk anymore—I waddle!" Such comments point out the loss of attractiveness that a woman can feel. All women have some beliefs about their physical appearance. During pregnancy their body image changes. Loss of attractiveness for many means loss of sex appeal. If a woman feels a strong loss, she will be very self-conscious about how others look at her and about comments others make. If she has a negative attitude about herself, she will color others' remarks to fit her own. A woman needs to start with her own acceptance of these changes, to accept them as normal and praise God for them. She needs reassurance at this time, and a husband's reassurance is vital. Some women like their body more during pregnancy. A woman can find beauty in her new shape. Positive comments shared with her husband may help him to respond in the manner desired.

Responses to the Christian Marriage and Family Survey

1. There are more married women—with children—in the work force than ever before. Do you think this has had a harmful effect on family life?

Yes, 92 percent

No, 8 percent

2. Would you approve if the wife were the main breadwinner and the husband took responsibility for the house and children?

Yes, 22 percent

No, 78 percent

3. Which of the following has the greatest influence on the general development of children under age 12?

5 percent—Friends   (3)

1.5 percent—Organized activities (sports, etc.)   (4)

23 percent—Television   (2)

0 percent—Books

1 percent—Church

1 percent—Teachers

67 percent—Parents   (1)

1 percent—Brothers and sisters

0 percent—Other relatives

0 percent—Others

4. At which point is it no longer necessary for the mother to remain at home?

a. Shortly after birth, 2.4 percent

b. When the youngest child enters preschool, 9 percent

c. When the youngest child enters grade school, 30 percent

d. When the youngest child enters junior high school, 7 percent

e. When the youngest child enters high school, 9 percent

f. When the youngest child enters college, 29 percent

g. Mother should always remain at home, 12 percent

Notes

All material quoted is used by permission.

1. "What's Happening to the American Family?" *Better Homes and Gardens*, 1978, pp. 62,69,88,89.

2. "Christian Marriage and Family Life Survey" (Denver: Christian Counseling and Enrichment, 1979).

3. Lee Salk and Rita Kramer, *How to Raise a Human Being* (New York: Random House, Inc., 1969), pp. 29,30.
4. Anfela Barron McBride, *The Growth and Development of Mothers* (New York: Harper & Row Publishers, Inc., 1974), pp. 30,31.
5. Elizabeth A. Hambrick-Stowe, *Expecting: A Christian Exploration of Pregnancy and Childbirth* (Valley Forge, PA: Judson Press, 1979), pp. 40,41.
6. Lyn Delli Quadri and Kati Breckenridge, *Mother Care* (Los Angeles: J.P. Taveher, 1978), p. 9.
7. Tracy Hotchner, *Pregnancy and Childbirth: The Complete Guide for a New Life* (New York: Avon Books, 1979), p. 158.

What Does a Father Do?

Both father and mother share in creating a new life, but they do not always share parenting roles beyond conception. During pregnancy the mother anticipates her future role through the development of the baby inside her, medical examinations, baby showers, and other activities. The father usually does not become involved until the child is born, when he suddenly realizes how unprepared he is to be a father and wonders what his role is or should be. Certainly it involves more than cooperating in conception and assisting at childbirth.

In her book *Fathering*, Maureen Green defined the traditional role of the father: "To the question 'What is father for?' many families would answer in one word: money. Millions still maintain their whole way of life, the ownership of their house and car, the clothes they wear and the holidays they enjoy on the income of one individual, the husband and father. Such families' whole standard of living reflects father's competence as a provider. Many thousands of other women and children also see father primarily as a provider because they are not provided for. They are bitterly aware that the reason they do not enjoy many things that others have is that no man makes it his job to see that they get them.

"Although the world we live in is fast changing shape, enough of the old patriarchal structure remains for the fatherless still to be at sore material disadvantage. The fatherless child is worse housed, worse fed, worse clothed, worse educated and worse supervised than the child who knows his father is around and taking an interest in the family. While making do without father, such children also see less of mother than others do; she has to be out and about, not only earning the family income, but dealing with every detail of their lives, from getting the new car license to hiring the camping equipment for the rare weekend in the country. So monotonously do the fatherless turn up in the poverty and social-deprivation statistics that psychologists and social workers attempting to come to grips with and define the specific characteristics of fatherlessness find themselves bogged down among the basic questions of survival that the poor have always had to face. Experts who have tried to write about the fatherless come up against the same problem. As Margaret Wynn was forced to confess at the beginning of her book *Fatherless Families,* 'Many of the consequences of fatherlessness discussed in this study are primarily the consequences of poverty.' To lose his father is the worst bit of bad luck, from the material point of view, that can happen to a child today. It is possible to ensure against father dying, which was the chief misfortune of the last century. But there is no way to ensure against divorce or separation, which is the disaster that removes father today.

"It may seem that if father is still so crucially important in terms of material support, no more need be said."[1]

WHAT DO YOU THINK?

1. Using several adjectives, describe your own father.

2. (Husband) What are your greatest concerns about becoming a father?

(Wife) What are your greatest concerns about your husband becoming a father?

3. (Husband) Describe specifically what you see yourself doing as a father.

(Wife) Describe specifically what you see your husband doing as a father.

4. (Husband) What are your reasons for wanting to be a father?

(Wife) What are your husband's reasons for wanting to be a father?

The Father's Role

It is important to consider both your own motives for becoming a father and your concerns about this new role. How do you know what kind of father you will become? One way is to reminisce about your own childhood and the relationship you experienced with your own father. Your memories may help you decide what areas of your life you would like to strengthen to function best as a father. What kind of man was your father? What qualities in his life do you desire in your own life? How did you father express his feelings toward you? How did the way he expressed feelings affect you? How will you express your feelings toward your child? What fathers did you or do you know that you admire? For what reasons? What difficulties have you noticed them experiencing?

Preparing for fatherhood is vital, but fatherhood is a job in our society for which there is no formal or informal training. Studies have indicated that an inadequate father may be worse than no father at all. Father passes on impressions, facets of his own personality, and a number of mental attitudes to his children.

What guidance does the Word of God give us concerning the role of the father? In the Old Testament the father was the founder and ruler of the family. "For I have chosen him, in order that he may command his children and his household after him to keep the way of the Lord by doing righteousness and justice; in order that the Lord may bring upon Abraham what He has spoken about him" (Gen. 18:19).

The father was the center of family strength, safety, and survival. The Bible depicts fathers as teachers of their children and leaders of the family's spiritual life. The father was one who loved his children (see Gen. 37:4) but sometimes had to rebuke them (see Gen. 34:30). He instructed them (see Prov. 1:8), befriended them (see Jer. 3:4), exhorted and comforted them (see 1 Thess. 2:11), and attempted to give them a proper upbringing (see Eph. 6:4). Nurturing as mentioned in this passage means to nourish—to provide optimal care for the children, not just enough to keep them alive.

Jewish fathers delighted in their sons but they also disciplined (see Prov. 3:12) and controlled them (see 1 Tim. 3:12). Fathers pitied their children's sufferings (see Ps. 103:13) and grieved over their folly (see Prov. 17:25).

A father was one who could be depended upon to deal honorably with his children and never cheat them. He always gave them the best gifts in his possession (see Matt. 7:11) provided for them (see 2 Cor. 12:14).

Paul likened himself to a good father: "For you know how, like a father with his children, we exhorted each one of you and encouraged you and charged you to lead a life worthy of God, who calls you into his own kingdom and glory" (1 Thess. 2:11,12, *RSV*).

The authors of *Fathering a Son,* Paul Heidebrecht and Jerry Rohrbach, described the biblical teaching on fatherhood in this way: "Becoming a father is a spiritual event for the Christian man. He recognizes that fatherhood is a calling. It is a God-given vocation, not unlike being a missionary, preacher, or teacher. To be a father is to play a major role in God's plan for His people, particularly in the teaching and training of children in the way of the Lord (Deuteronomy 6:4-9). The Old Testament shows how God uses parents, especially father, to transmit the values and truths of His Word to the following generation (Psalm 78:1-8; Isaiah 38:19). In the New Testament, the father is given responsibility for the spiritual nurture of his family (Eph. 6:4).

"The effective father recognizes that fatherhood is a mandate from God, and he accepts the responsibilities and privileges it brings. He makes a major investment of his time and energy in this calling. He knows there will be enjoyable and difficult times, but he knows also that the God who called him to this unique ministry will sustain him through it.

"In his book *The Effective Father*, Gordon MacDonald uses the analogy of an orchestra conductor to describe the father's pacesetting role. In the analogy, the father is the conductor, his family is the orchestra, and God is the composer of the music. The father's task is to make sure the 'orchestra' plays the music the way the 'composer' wrote it. In other words, his job is to make sure the members of his family are living the way God intends for them to live.

"How does the effective father set this kind of pace?

—By expecting obedience from his children and following through to make sure he gets it.

—By protecting his children from harmful influences and supervising their character development.

—By developing good habits in his children's lives.

—By dealing directly with sinful or immature behavior.

—By teaching God's standards for living, as found in the Bible (Deuteronomy 11:18-19).

—By living before his children the kind of life he wants them to live (Joshua 24:14-15).

"All this develops a pace of life that his children can learn to follow."[2]

God gave us examples of how to respond to our children and how not to. In 2 Samuel 13, we read about David and his son Absalom. Absalom had killed his half-brother for violating his sister. He fled and left the area for some time. Finally, David became convicted about the treatment of one of his sons as an exile, and he gave these orders: "Behold now, I will surely do this thing; go therefore, bring back the young man, Absalom" (2 Sam. 14:21). But because Absalom had committed such an awful sin, he added, "Let him turn to his own house, and let him not see my face" (v. 24). Notice the rejection by the father. Absalom went to his own house, and did not see the king's face for two more years. David forgave Absalom only in a limited way, but he continued to reject him. "You may come back into town, but I don't want to see you."

Later Absalom led a rebellion against his father and Absalom was killed in the rebellion. David's unresolved intense feelings were expressed in 2 Samuel 18:33: "And the king was deeply moved and went up to the chamber over the gate and wept. And thus he said as he walked, 'O my son Absalom, my son, my son Absalom! Would I had died instead of you, O Absalom, my son, my son!' " David finally accepted his son, but it was too late. Absalom had lived there for several years, not knowing that his father loved him because David did not accept him as he was. It is so easy for a father to reject his child for doing a displeasing act.

A positive example of fathering is the story of the forgiving father. In Luke 15 we read how the son went off, taking what belonged to him. He squandered it all and ended up living with the pigs and eating what they ate. One day he decided that he would get up and go home: "And he got up and came to his father. But while he was still a long way off, his father saw him, and felt compassion for him, and ran and embraced him, and kissed him" (v. 20). Sometimes as parents we sit and wait for the other to come to us. We don't make the first move. We seem to be saying, "You have to convince me that you're sorry and that you want forgiveness and that you're going to be a changed person. I must have a guarantee that you will never do that again." There are no guarantees. To forgive a person or to love a person, we have to be willing to run the risk of trusting him or her and being hurt again. The risk is always there, but if we don't take it what is our alternative?

In the story Jesus told, the father brought the best robe, the honor robe, and put it on the son. He brought out the fattened calf and said, "Let us eat and be merry; for this son of mine was dead, and has come to life again; he was lost, and has been found." This was a time of rejoicing. Forgiveness was complete. This story shows how fathers should respond to their children and demonstrate God's presence in their own lives.

WHAT DO YOU THINK?

1. Look up Ephesians 4:32 and Colossians 3:12,13. Which of the characteristics listed are most difficult for you to exhibit consistently in your life?

2. Which of these characteristics are most essential in your role as a parent?

3. Discuss with your spouse how you assist each other in developing these characteristics in your life, especially in your parenting roles.

Preparing for Fatherhood

What can you do to prepare for fatherhood?

First, examine and clarify your own feelings about being a father. Was your wife's pregnancy a surprise or planned for? What are your feelings about it? Earlier we discussed remembering your own experiences with your father and how they affected you. This, too, is part of the preparation process.

Second, put yourself in situations where you can care for infants and interact with children. This doesn't mean you will be attracted to children any more than you were before. Fathers seem to be attracted basically just to their own children.

Third, learn about the process of pregnancy. It will help you feel involved. Help your wife choose an obstetrician. During the initial visit, the two of you can determine if the doctor is the one you will feel comfortable with. It is important for you to hear his instructions. Just being there will ease your mind about your impending fatherhood. Your role will definitely be that of a support system—keeping track of what the doctor says to you and listening carefully to your wife's explanation of what he tells her when she sees the doctor by herself.

Be sure to talk with your doctor about your wife's physical symptoms and mood swings. Don't kid her about changing size and shape. During pregnancy a wife needs her husband's calm support at all times, even during these mood swings. In addition to sensitivity, fears, and depression, she may withdraw her emotional support from you as she becomes more attentive to the baby.

"You must realize that this is usually just a temporary situation; you have not lost her affection and you are not in competition with the child. If, however, her withdrawal from you is very strong and you are constantly feeling ignored, this could be a danger sign. Her withdrawal or even resentment of you may become a permanent thing, either induced by pregnancy or by some problem in your marriage. It may go away temporarily but may surface again during the next crisis or strain on your marriage."[3]

Any arrangements you can make—such as the hospital appointments—will be helpful. If you feel she is tiring herself out, be sure to speak up. Praying for and with your wife regularly will be appreciated especially at this time.

Husbands differ in their response toward pregnancy. Their reactions can be classified into three categories.

"1. There is the husband who readily and eagerly accepts the responsibilities and fulfillment of being a family man. Such a husband considers the pregnancy a gift and becomes very close to his wife.

"2. The totally career-oriented husband often regards prospective fatherhood as a burden that interferes with his job responsibilities. Such a husband tries hard to reaffirm all his old habits and denies the need for change in his way of living. For instance, he may want to take his pregnant wife on long camping trips and otherwise act 'normally.'

"3. The emotionally immature husband approaches fatherhood casually. Often this husband is frightened at the prospect of having to support a wife and a child, where previously he had been financially dependent on others. His main problem is making the transition from carefree adolescent to responsible adult. His wife's pregnancy is frequently accompanied by marital crisis and conflict with relatives.''[4]

Any man may feel the strain of pregnancy. Some men even increase their sports activities to show they are physically and mentally young. Others may experience minor psychosomatic complaints, and some exhibit deviant social behaviors.

Some men even develop physical symptoms of pregnancy. This is the time to saturate yourself with information from knowledgeable fathers, your obstetrician, books, and magazines. Natural childbirth classes are a must, and your presence in the labor and delivery rooms is vital in establishing a close relationship among the three of you. Be sure to read *Father Power* by Henry Biller and Dennis Meredith. Share with your wife what you learn through your own study.

Becoming a father is a life-changing experience. Your emotions will run a wide range. Some of your hopes and expectations will be met, and others may not be met. Dave Ferreira, a friend of mine who is a young father, graphically described his experience during the birth of his son. This account sums up beautifully one of life's greatest moments.

"He stood silently alone dressed in his delivery garb, feeling as dependent and helpless as a roofer on a two-story house who has lost his ladder and hammer. The four white walls entombed him. The words of the doctors he had heard only moments before flashed through his mind, one sticking out like a neon sign in a ghost town—'operate.'

"Numbness spread throughout his body and mind, partially from the exhausting twenty hours of constant labor, but also from the fear of losing his child or wife. Painful memories of a lost mother in childhood bombarded his soul. The painful thought of the exhaustion he saw in his wife's face and the long hours of pushing and never ending contractions were more than his mental processes could bear. And now the report that the child was transverse, they would probably need to operate, and he couldn't be with her. His emotions rose up and reached fever pitch, changing directions like a steel ball in a pinball machine. Anger, hurt, frustration, fear—all adding up to a bottomless pit of helplessness.

"Palms sweating, pacing the floor, a knot tying itself tighter and tighter in his stomach, he had nowhere to turn but to God. In the past he was so independent he could always get by with his own determination or with God's help, but now he was totally dependent. At first his mind raced, trying to think of all the right ways to appease and please a God who could turn a painful world around for him. Finally, he slowed long enough to sense that the God of the universe was at work, not on his child or wife, but on him. It was a time for building character, for trusting, for knowing God was God. Although the deep peace was there, the anxiety continued to strike in armor-piercing blows. The minutes seemed as hours of eternity.

"Finally, the word came—he could go in. The last effort was successful, they told him, and he half-consciously floated through the maze of halls to an eagerly waiting wife who cried as he took her head in his hands. The exhaustion of the previous hours was lifted as together they watched the delivery of their firstborn son. As much as he wanted to cry, tears would not come, for the emotions of the last minutes had left him numb. He could only smile and feel very small compared to a big God who had blessed him with a wife and child he treasured deeply.

"The task has now begun to allow God to develop character in himself so that he might be an example and tool in training his son. 'Lord, grant me your grace to be real enough to let my wife and son know me for who I am and to search for who they are, not assuming I already know. Help me to be the father you want me to be, following your examples of love through good times and bad. Give me the insight and strength to be able to discipline my child not from my needs, but for his good. And thank you for blessing me and finding me worthy in your Son to influence another's life so deeply "

WHAT'S YOUR PLAN?

1. Describe in detail what you need to do to prepare for parenthood.

2. List what you will be doing as preparation during the remaining time before your child's birth.

Notes

All material quoted is used by permission.
1. Maureen Green, *Fathering* (New York: McGraw-Hill Book Co., 1976), pp. 62,63.
2. Paul Heidebrecht and Jerry Rohrbach, *Fathering a Son* (Chicago: Moody Press, 1979), pp. 35,36.
3. Henry Biller and Dennis Meredith, *Father Power* (New York: Doubleday & Company, Inc., 1975), p. 31.
4. *Ibid.*, p. 40.

What's Up, Doc?

A new wind blowing in our modern society is bringing new attitudes about pregnancy and childbirth. Rules of even five years ago are changing, allowing more freedom and interaction for parents in the process of childbirth. Parents can make more decisions about the delivery and methods to be employed. Until recently men in this country have not been allowed to be present at the birth of their children. Even this tradition has changed in the last 10 to 15 years with the advent of "natural" childbirth and the preparation for birth provided by hospitals and classes across the country.

What kind of childbirth experience would you like to have? Can your doctor provide the necessary services? Maybe you don't know what is available. In this chapter we will discuss the doctor's role in childbirth and how you can get what you want at the time of delivery.

First, let's find out what the Scriptures teach about childbirth. Edith Deen, in her excellent book *Family Living in the Bible*, gives the following pictures of childbirth during biblical times:

"Though Israelite women in Egypt were said to have given birth easily (Exodus 1:19), as do many Bedouin women in Palestine today, the pains of childbirth were a common experience.

'Pain, as of a woman in travail' (Psalm 48:6) is mentioned often by the prophets: Isaiah (13:8; 21:3; 26:17), Jeremiah (4:31; 6:24; 13:21; 22:23; 50:43), and Hosea (13:13).

"Jesus expressed the feelings of mothers when He said, 'A woman when she is in travail hath sorrow, because her hour is come: but as soon as she is delivered of the child, she remembereth no more the anguish, for joy that a man is born into the world' (John 16:21).

"Midwives customarily assisted women in childbirth. These are so named in Genesis 35:17; 38:28 and Exodus 1:15-22. Such attendants, as in the story of Ichabod's mother (1 Samuel 4:20), were usually the older relatives and friends of the mother.

"After a baby was born he was washed, rubbed with salt which was believed to harden him, and wrapped in swaddling clothes, because of a false notion that movement would harm his arms and legs (Ezekiel 16:4). Almost immediately his mother gave him a name expressive of his personality, though sometimes the father named his children (Genesis 35:18).

"Seven children seem to have been the average number in the Hebrew family, as in these specified cases: 'the barren hath borne seven' (I Samuel 2:5) and 'she that hath borne seven languisheth' (Jeremiah 15:9). Seven daughters are once mentioned (Exodus 2:16) and seven sons are twice mentioned (Job 1:2 and Job 42:13).

"Mothers generally suckled their babies (I Samuel 1:21-23), but a wet nurse was occasionally employed (Exodus 2:7; II Kings 11:2). Isaiah speaks of the tender love of a mother for her nursling: 'Can a woman forget her sucking child, that she should not have compassion on the son of her womb?' (Isaiah 49:15).

"Birth was sometimes dangerous for mother and child. The Bible records two difficult deliveries in which the mothers died though their babies lived: Rachel (Genesis 35:16-20) and the un-named mother of Ichabod, already cited. Premature births are mentioned (Job 3:16, Psalm 58:8, Ecclesiastes 6:3). The death of an infant from accidental suffocation occurred during Solomon's reign (I Kings 3:19).

"For forty days after a son's birth and fifty days after a daughter's, a mother was considered ceremonially unclean. Before taking up her normal life again, she offered a sacrifice in the ritual of purification (Leviticus 12:2-8). Faithful to the old laws, Mary went up to Jerusalem forty days after the birth of Jesus to offer her sacrifice (Luke 2:22-24)."[1]

A Choice Is Not a Demand

Tracy Hotchner says the following regarding choices available to today's expectant parents:

"You have many options about where you will give birth and who will attend you. In order to decide what is the right setting for you—and what technical aids and attendants you do or do not want—you need to know the pros and cons of the available choices in childbirth. Your community may not offer all the possible options but *you can change that.* . . .

"Time is short. You're about to get pregnant or you already are, so you have to move quickly if you want to bring about change. . . . Because hospitals are profit-making institutions they *need your business:* they have to at least listen to you if they hope to get you or keep you as a customer. If you live in a 'one hospital town' the monopoly principle applies—if you have no 'hospital down the block' to turn to, then you haven't got as much leverage. The same is true on a lesser scale for doctors."[2]

Several principles must be applied to get the most out of the childbirth experience.

Whatever you desire, make sure you and your spouse agree before taking your request to the authority in charge. It can be very disconcerting to everyone involved if you and your spouse are asking for contradictory things. Ultimately the doctor will make the decision, which might not be what you wish. If you and your spouse disagree, pray about it and ask for the doctor's guidance.

If you have a question, the first person to discuss it with is your doctor—not parents, friends, *Red Book,* etc.

"Ask, and it shall be given to you; seek, and you shall find; knock, and it shall be opened to you" (Matt. 7:7). This is very practical advice for the expectant parent. Don't put everyone on the defensive with your fervor. The passage is clear: *don't* demand, chase, or break down doors. A gentle spirit will get you a lot further in dealing with the doctor or hospital.

Set objectives; don't waste people's time. Know what you want ahead of time. Explain concisely to the doctor what you want and why. He will listen.

Make your requests known early. Don't wait until you are in delivery to request a special anesthesia. If you and your doctor agree on special procedures, make sure they become part of your records. You may even want a copy to take to the hospital with you in case you arrive before your doctor or he is off duty and another doctor is on call in his place.

WHAT DO YOU THINK?

1. What are five expectations you have for your doctor?
    (1)

    (2)

    (3)

    (4)

    (5)

2. List five things you think your spouse would desire during the birth of your child:
    (1)

    (2)

    (3)

(4)

(5)

3. What would you be willing to do to meet your spouse's desires?

4. List five of your own desires:
   (1)

   (2)

   (3)

   (4)

   (5)

5. Next to each desire in questions 2 and 4 identify who has control of meeting each expectation; use the following code: I—I (yourself); S—spouse; D—doctor; O—other.

6. When will you discuss your desires with the person responsible for their fulfillment?

7. How would you feel if these desires were not met?

What Choices?

The choices available to you depend on the area of the country and size of the community in which you live. Many larger areas of this country provide progressive hospitals and more alternatives to birth than do some of the smaller communities. Do not feel badly if you do not have all the choices available to you. What is most important is the health and safety of mother and child.

We have listed some of the choices that may be available. We are not advocating a specific method or discussing pros or cons, but merely providing the information. If you want further information, read Hotchner's book, *Pregnancy and Childbirth: The Complete Guide for a New Life*. Always consult your doctor as the final authority.

Alternate Birth Center (ABC)—provides a setting similar to the home bedroom, emphasizing the normality of pregnancy but with complete medical services available. The stay at the center is normally short (6 to 24 hours), and the cost is lower than for traditional hospital care.

Analgesia—any drug that reduces pain or is used to relax the mother. All drugs taken during labor reach the baby.

Anesthesia (local)—provides numbness and pain-killing to a specific area, allowing the mother to be fully awake. Anesthesia is used for women with low pain tolerance and for women who are not prepared for natural childbirth.

Cesarean delivery—surgical removal of the infant. One out of eight births is accomplished in this manner. It may be possible for the husband to participate if the cesarean birth is planned and he has taken preparatory classes.

Childbirth classes—whatever the name of the method, the goal is the same—to relax the body, avoiding anxiety—prolonging the ability to endure the contractions. Not only is the mother taught the basics of relaxing, but the husband or coach learns how to become an integral part of the process, providing support and creating a oneness between the couple. To find a childbirth class or a certified nurse or midwife, consult your doctor or write to the International Childbirth Education Association (P.O. Box 5852, Milwaukee, Wisconsin 53220) or call your local American Red Cross chapter or YWCA. Classes begin about the seventh month of pregnancy and consist of lecture, demonstration, films, and hospital tour.

Other choices that may appeal to you, which depend on your doctor's discretion, include home birth, midwives, friends attending birth, siblings attending birth, fetal heart monitoring, the Leboyer method, use of forceps and induction of labor.

WHAT DO YOU THINK?

How do you know you are pregnant? What are the signs? What would you do first? Try the following agree-disagree quiz.

	Husband		Wife	
	A	D	A	D
1. A woman experiences only physical changes during pregnancy.	☐	☐	☐	☐
2. A missed period is the last sign of pregnancy.	☐	☐	☐	☐
3. There are several accurate ways to determine a baby's sex.	☐	☐	☐	☐
4. The mother determines the sex of the baby.	☐	☐	☐	☐
5. Morning sickness occurs during the entire pregnancy.	☐	☐	☐	☐
6. The first thing you should do when you become pregnant is put yourself under a doctor's supervision.	☐	☐	☐	☐

If you disagreed with numbers 1 through 5 and agreed with number 6, you did very well.

If you have any questions to discuss with your doctor, write them down to keep them fresh in your mind.

What Do You Mean You're Pregnant?

The most noticeable sign that a woman is pregnant is the cessation of her menstrual flow. If she is more than 10 days late, there is a good possibility she may be pregnant. There are a number of other reasons for a late or missing period, so a doctor should be consulted as soon as possible. An easy laboratory test, conducted about 13 days after the missed period, can determine effectively if a woman is pregnant.

Another option available is the early pregnancy test for home use. After waiting 12 years for our first child, Rita and I had decided that we wanted to share the birth experience as totally as possible. On the day after Easter, 1978 we performed our own early pregnancy test, which takes two hours. After running the test Rita left for work not knowing the results. I probably checked that little vial 10 times during the next two hours. When the small dark ring appeared at the vial's bottom, I was elated and had the pleasure of calling Rita to say, ''We're pregnant.'' This test was immediately followed up with a visit to our doctor for professional confirmation.

Rita and I found that pregnancy and childbirth afforded us a unique experience of growing spiritual oneness. At no other time in our marriage did that oneness become so alive and real. Since the birth of our daughter, that oneness continues to bond us and continues to grow.

Other normal symptoms of early pregnancy include:

Frequent urination caused by the pressure of the growing uterus upon the bladder

Morning sickness—a queasy sensation that may last throughout the day and into the night. A pregnant woman may be nauseated and feel like vomiting, but it usually subsides in 6 to 12 weeks. A good aid for morning sickness is to eat a piece of dry toast or a soda cracker before getting out of bed in the morning.

Fatigue. The woman's body may need more sleep. During pregnancy 8 to 10 hours of sleep per night are needed with some naps and rest during the day.

Body changes. Breasts increase in size and become tender to the touch and firmer. Nipples darken in color and widen. Skin tone may change (called the ''mask of pregnancy''). A dark line may appear on the middle of the stomach, called *linea negra* (black line). These marks usually fade after birth. Stretch marks may appear on the breasts, abdomen and thighs as the skin stretches to accommodate the new fullness of the body. In all likelihood the stretch marks will remain after the birth of the baby.

Growing abdominal area (tummy). By the fifth month, the uterus will have expanded to reach the navel and the woman will "look" pregnant. She will begin to "show" by the third month.

Elephants are pregnant for two years. Fortunately, human pregnancy does not last nearly that long; it only seems so. The average length of pregnancy is about 280 days, or 40 weeks from the first day of the last menstrual period. The length can vary greatly; a range of 240 to 300 days is still considered normal. Don't be upset if the baby arrives "early" or "late"; God has control. Some babies require more time to develop; some require less. Don't count on your "due" date; it is only an approximation. The probability of a baby arriving on its due date is only three percent. To calculate your due date, add seven days to the date of the beginning of the last period and then add nine months.

> Example: *Last period started*   *Due Date*
> November 20 +7 days + 9 months =   August 27

If you have any questions you would like to discuss with your doctor, write them down while they are still fresh in your mind.

Selecting a Doctor

Marcia Colman Morton, in her *Pregnancy Notebook,* has this to say about selecting a doctor:

"If you don't already have a regular gynecologist/obstetrician, finding one is your first pregnancy job. You want the best qualified, most experienced doctor there is. Probably your general practitioner or family internist will refer you to his most trusted obstetrical colleague. Or your mother or older sister or friend-who-had-a-baby-last-year will urge you to get *her* wonderful doctor to oversee your pregnancy and delivery. You can also call your local county medical society, or go right to the best hospital in your community and ask for a list of the doctors on the obstetrics staff.

"Whichever guide you follow, the important thing is to be sure your obstetrician's medical credentials are unimpeachable. His postgraduate training as a specialist should have been at a first-class hospital and he should be on the staff of one of the top hospitals in town. Check him out with a doctor you already know and trust or with your local medical society. Then, on your very first visit, decide if you feel comfortable with him; if you find him kind and sympathetic and compatible—because you and he will be collaborators on a months-long project.

"I, for instance, did not feel at ease with the first obstetrician to whom I was referred. He was an excellent doctor but some of the attitudes he expressed seemed old-fashioned to me. I didn't feel I would be able to talk freely with him through all my visits. So I asked *everyone* about obstetricians. When four separate women all recommended the same pair of doctors (gynecologists often work as a duet so that one of them is always sure to be available when your baby decides to be born), I felt that was pretty impressive. First I got my internist's medical approval; then I made an appointment, found them very congenial and never regretted my switch."[3]

Tracy Hotchner shares these thoughts about doctors with expectant parents:

"Patients put unrealistic demands on doctors, who are expected to have all the answers, know everything, and be totally responsible. As women start taking more responsibility for their own bodies it's going to be easier on everyone, but in the meantime doctors are still expected to know and do it all. Giving up traditional procedures in obstetrics may be frightening to doctors because it leaves them hanging—the tradition is taken away as a bulwark and there is nothing to replace it.

"Doctors did not design the dangers in being alive . . . they want to minimize them (this is one reason they fall back on traditional thinking). No two labors are alike. The physical and emotional intensity of labor and delivery is awesome. It is still not understood what triggers labor and often all the machines and medications cannot control it. Yet doctors are nevertheless expected to know what is going on; to be in charge; to be responsible for the outcome of a perfect baby.

"We should keep in mind that doctors may also feel frustration, pressure, guilt, depression, and strain. Being a doctor is a complex and difficult task, perhaps even harder than some doctors recognize. Do not be angry with a doctor who may be rigid—be compassionate toward a person who has been channeled into playing God by his fellow-men and women.

"The one danger is a doctor who practices medicine with his ego. There are doctors who have gotten so caught up in the role, and people's expectations that they actually come to believe that they do have all the answers. Beware of any doctor, in or out of the hospital, who does not separate his ego and his medicine. An example would be any doctor who will not listen to any point of view that differs from his own, who refuses to consider any procedure he is not familiar with.

"Doctors are not bad people, although some of them may be. Doctors are not great people, although some of them may be. Mostly doctors are decent people under a lot of pressure trying to do the best job they can."[4]

Choosing a doctor should not be taken lightly. This decision should be based on wisdom and discernment. How would you describe wisdom? Derek Kidner describes wisdom as including at least five facets:[5]

Instruction or training—this is not a static learning situation but on-the-job training that you will receive in preparing for parenthood. Your doctor needs to be able to provide or point you to this training.

Understanding or insight (whose root is to *discern*)—this is the ability to approach parenthood and parenting with good sense.

Wise dealing—make your dealings with doctors and hospitals successful. Use good sense; be practical.

Discretion—be a godly man who in the best sense is a man of affairs. Plan ahead; know the questions ahead of time. Proverbs says, "The prudent sees the evil and hides himself, but the naive go on, and are punished for it" (22:3).

Knowledge—it is the wise man's responsibility to gain through learning.

Becoming a parent is a time of preparing, a time to grow more wise and to demonstrate wisdom bestowed by God. If you approach the doctor as a wise man and woman looking for wisdom, trusting wisdom, you will be accepted as wise and not as a fool.

The Doctor's Office

You suspect you're pregnant, you've chosen a doctor, and now you arrive at his office. Now what?

The first thing you can expect is for the doctor or nurse to take a medical history, which may include the following: your past health; parents' health; grandparents' health; husband's health; kind of work you do; miscarriages/abortions; history of previous pregnancies; menstruation—age of onset, regular, last period; medications; alcohol/smoking; illnesses; anemia.

After the medical history, you will be weighed and have your blood pressure checked. You will be asked for a urine specimen and a blood sample will be taken, or they will arrange for you to visit a lab.

The doctor will examine you. He will check your eyes, ears, nose, and throat, looking for signs of infection. He will check your chest, breasts, and abdomen. The doctor will conduct an internal pelvic examination to feel the uterus, checking its size, shape, and position. This is done to help determine how far along the pregnancy has progressed. When he has finished, the doctor will discuss your general care and health during pregnancy. He should discuss the following: food; rest; sleep; weight; recreation; problems; care of your teeth; clothing; work; exercise; costs; schedule of visits.

The doctor will probably want you to see a dentist early in pregnancy. Tell the dentist on the phone you are pregnant so he can take precautions to protect you from anesthesia and x-rays. The baby's formation requires much calcium, and the loss of calcium you normally use yourself to maintain your teeth may cause dental problems.

Notify your doctor immediately if you have any sign of the following problems: bleeding from the vagina; severe nausea or vomiting; fever or chills; swelling of feet, ankles, legs, hands; abdominal pain; continuing headache; decrease in urine; sudden gush of water from the vagina; pain or burning when passing urine.

Any medication, prescription or non-prescription, unless the doctor has prescribed it, should be avoided, including the following:[6] antibiotics; baking soda; laxatives; digestive aids; diet pills; tranquilizers; aspirin and other pain relievers; nose drops or sprays; Also: x-rays, alcohol; smoking; raw meat; new cats and litter boxes.

The Doctor and the Father

Fathers traditionally have not had a significant role in child-bearing. Mom went to the hospital to tough it out alone while Dad paced the fathers' waiting room with a box of pink-and-blue-banded cigars to pass out. Today's natural childbirth emphasis places Dad in a private position on the team. He can now be an active participant rather than a passive bystander.

Fathers need to take the active role from the beginning. One way Rita and I decided to make our pregnancy an experience in oneness was to participate together in her examinations. Many of the questions fathers may have about pregnancy and child care are answered during the fathers' classes. The husband learns how to be a coach and how to help his wife during labor and how to care for newborn babíes. It is important for the father to visit with the doctor early in the pregnancy to clarify his role and to understand what is expected of the father and the doctor by each other.

Pregnancy and Sex

One area the husband may be interested in as well as the wife, but may be fearful to talk about with each other let alone with the doctor, is sexual relations during pregnancy. Fear not, you don't have to stop making love when you're pregnant.

Dr. Louis A. Gentile has the following to say about sex during pregnancy in his article, "Sex and the Expectant Couple":

"The subject of sex *in* pregnancy is still relatively unexplored and undiscussed, even though sex is how it all began. It is almost as if it is perfectly acceptable to have sexual relations and to achieve conception—but somehow it isn't right to continue after that. Most books and manuals on childbearing concentrate on preparing expectant parents, especially the mother-to-be, for the events of pregnancy and for labor and delivery. Although there may be some mention of sexual relations, the emphasis is on getting ready for parenthood.

"This is unfortunate, because pregnancy can represent a new opportunity for intimacy and romance—made all the more fulfilling with the knowledge of a new life on the way. For couples who have actively sought the pregnancy after ceasing to practice family planning, it can bring a new sense of freedom and a release from the pressure of trying to conceive. Pregnancy can also create problems in sexual relations, but these difficulties should be faced with the same honesty and tenderness that a couple needs to bring to their sexual life generally."[7]

In the normal, healthy pregnancy God has given a high degree of protection to the infant forming within its mother, and with very few exceptions intercourse during pregnancy can bring no harm to the infant. We have already discussed some problems that require the immediate attention of your doctor; the presence of any of these problems may also affect sexual relations during pregnancy.

Certain changes taking place can cause or result in sexual problems between a pregnant couple. Dr. Gentile describes the following:

Emotional Changes—a wide range of moods, both up and down. Some women become more loving, tender, and outgoing than ever. Others tend to withdraw and become self-absorbed. Both changes are normal. Feelings on the wife's part that her husband it not involved in the pregnancy and is not sharing her feelings or involvement are also normal. The husband may also experience a number of emotional changes, including feeling a loss of his wife's love or fear of the new role of father that he faces.

Physical changes—especially in later pregnancy. Some couples have a difficult time adjusting to the physical changes and awkwardness that pregnancy poses.

Fear of harming the baby falls into the category of myths. Many doctors still forbid intercourse during the last four to six weeks of pregnancy as a matter of custom and concern about infection. Some couples fear that orgasm may bring about early labor. Dr. Gentile says:

"Only a few studies have been done on this subject, and the tests have been inconclusive. The likelihood is that premature labor is caused by a number of different factors, and in a normal pregnancy it would not be initiated by orgasm alone."[8]

Awkwardness is another factor that may affect the couple's ability to perform. The enlargement and tenderness of the woman's breasts may cause her to withdraw from her husband's touch or kisses.

"The important thing to keep in mind is that pregnancy is

clearly a time of great emotional upheaval. Understanding between the two partners is the key to maintaining (and improving) their sexual relations. The frequency of intercourse will change; positions in lovemaking will have to be modified, to reduce discomfort.

"In the early stage of pregnancy, the positions generally favored by both partners can be maintained as before. As pregnancy advances, many couples will gradually stop using the male superior position, if this is the one they have adopted most often in the past. There is no danger to the baby, but it avoids placing undue weight on the woman's abdomen and sensitive breasts. The female superior positions, or side-by-side position, will probably be more comfortable. This is also a good time to experiment with new positions, a time when a couple's ingenuity in this respect is challenged.

"As in other aspects of their life together, good judgment and a certain amount of moderation should be the guide. And, of course, a concern for each other's feelings and sexual needs should always be present."[9]

The Baby's Doctor

The doctor who cares for your child is just as important as the doctor who delivers the infant, perhaps even more important. The obstetrician cares for the mother and the unborn child until birth, approximately nine months. A pediatrician will be your child's doctor for maybe the next 18 years or longer. He will be at your beck and call night and day, through chicken pox, colds, flu, cuts, scrapes, broken bones, and disasters. Who will he be? How will you choose that doctor? Some communities are small enough to make it simple: there is only one doctor. But most communities offer a number of practitioners.

WHAT DO YOU THINK?

Take a few minutes with your spouse to discuss the following items. Write down your answers for future reference.

1. How will you choose a doctor for your child?

Where will you get names of doctors to consider?

What should his qualifications be?

What do you need to know to feel comfortable with him personally and professionally?

2. List at least 10 questions you would like to ask the doctor and state at least one reason for asking each question.

3. When will you discuss these questions with the doctor—before he is chosen or after you have decided he is to be your doctor? What will you do if you are not happy with his answers to your questions?

There are many ways to choose a pediatrician: pick a name from the phone book, call your local medical society, ask your family doctor for a recommendation, or ask friends. In our case, we were given several names by our doctor, and the same names kept coming up in recommendations from friends. Rita and I made a list of questions that we wanted answered, picked five pediatricians we had been referred to, and called them for personal appointments. What an experience! Two doctors refused to talk with us. One doctor wanted to charge for an office visit and then asked us to leave. Two doctors graciously consented to see us, one during his lunch hour and the other at the end of his day. We were glad their patients came first. Our final choice came down to equal qualifications, similar facilities and fees, but the difference was in personality and an extra demonstration of care. The pediatrician we chose had a partner. We asked our doctor the following questions which we are including for your use. You are welcome to add to them, change them, or throw them out, but we feel they have been useful and have prevented many misunderstandings.

1. *What is your professional training and background in pediatrics?* Our doctor likes working with children and went into medicine with pediatrics in mind. He was well trained and served a pediatric internship.

2. *What are your hospital affiliations?* If there is a problem, how far will you have to drive? Our doctor is associated with two hospitals which have large emergency rooms and one that is also attached to our local children's hospital.

3. *What are your office hours?* When can you get hold of the doctor? Do his hours fit your work schedules?

4. *What are your fees?* Can you afford him? What about insurance payments? How are they handled? Remember that fees change—always up!

5. *If you were looking for a pediatrician, what would you expect in that man or woman?* Write down his expectations.

6. *Do you fulfill your expectations?* After a long thoughtful pause, our doctor looked at us and said, "Yes, I do. I wouldn't be here if I didn't." His confidence certainly came across.

7. *Could you give three positive characteristics of your practice?* He told us (1) about his capable staff and their length of

service. Our doctor was the newest staff member. (2) The difference in ages of the two doctors in the practice—age and experience versus youth and modern technology—complement each other. He cited (3) availability and convenience as another positive characteristic.

8. *What is the major weakness in your practice?* "The age difference between me and my partner" he said. Sometimes it causes personal conflicts because our doctor attempts to be more open and communicative. We appreciated his honesty.

9. *How can we help to prevent this weakness from becoming a problem for us?* "Don't ever be afraid to ask questions and ask for clarification of our procedures. Be firm with my partner and show you are interested in your child. He will take the time to discuss the situation with you."

10. *What is your philosophy of child rearing?* "Get to know your doctor." What if you and your physician disagree? Will you be able to work things out?

11. *When will you arrive at the hospital?*

12. *Describe your procedure during and after the delivery. What are our options?* This is a good time to discuss your desires and needs. Get them into the record. Is he willing to work with you?

13. *What do we need to know about feeding?* My wife cannot nurse and feared being put down by the doctor. He went out of his way to make her feel comfortable, clarified her situation, and talked about several special procedures to deal with some special medical problems (for example, allergies).

14. *If the office is closed, what do we do?* I would rather know now than during an emergency.

15. *When do we call you?* Our doctor told us, "You are to call me *whenever* you are feeling uncomfortable with your child." This is the answer that sold us on our doctor.

16. *How often do we bring the child in? Why?*

17. *What about immunizations?* They keep complete records and automatically schedule immunizations with regular visits. You could go to a county health department for free.

18. *Will we receive progress reports?* "The chart is open to you. I will keep you posted of developments and problems with each visit."

19. *How much time do we get with you? Are you punctual?*
20. *What do you want to know from us as parents?*
21. *How can we best help you?*

WHAT'S YOUR PLAN?

1. Describe the kind of pregnancy and delivery you would like to have.

2. What will the doctor have to be willing to do to provide the kind of care you want?

3. List the potential doctors you would like to use.

4. Describe how you will arrive at a decision. List at least five criteria you will use.

5. List any fears you may have or think your spouse may have. Decide who will help you with your fears.

6. My final decision for a doctor is:

7. My doctor's address is:

His telephone number is:

My first appointment is:

8. My dental appointment is:

9. My pediatrician is:

10. Questions I need to have answered (Write them down now before you forget.):

Notes

All material quoted used by permission.
1. Edith Deen, *Family Living in the Bible* (Old Tappan, NJ: Fleming H. Revell Company, 1969), pp. 95,96. (Spire edition by Pyramid Publications.)
2. Tracy Hotchner, *Pregnancy and Childbirth: The Complete Guide for a New Life* (New York: Avon Books, 1979), pp. 202,203.
3. Marcia Morton, *Pregnancy Notebook* (New York: Bantam Books, 1972), pp. 18,19.
4. Hotchner, pp. 294,295.
5. Derek Kidner, *Proverbs: An Introduction and Commentary* (London: Tyndale Press, 1964), pp. 36,37.
6. National Foundation of the March of Dimes (leaflet).
7. Louis A. Gentile, M.D., "Sex and the Expectant Couple," *Expecting*, (Winter, 1979/80), pp. 24,26.
8. *Ibid.*, pp. 26,27.
9. *Ibid.*, p. 28.

Countdown for Delivery

One of the grandest experiences many women have during their lifetime is giving birth to a new life, to a new creation, to a new child. The picture is one of ecstasy, beauty, and love. In the past, women experienced this event alone—without the father, and usually under anesthesia. Today both mother and father are encouraged to share the experience and prepare for it beforehand.

Preparing for Childbirth

Today's "natural" childbirth or prepared childbirth emphasizes the need for knowledge and learning and places responsibility on both the mother and the father at the time of delivery. Granted, a father cannot give birth to a child but, as coach or leader of the team, he supervises the labor his wife is undergoing. Through his supervision and the conditioning his wife has undergone prior to delivery, she is able to relax; and by relaxing she can counteract normal tension which arises out of fear of the unknown.

Lee Salk, noted American child psychologist, has this to say about anticipating the unknown and learning all you can beforehand:

"I can easily imagine how you must react listening to someone ecstatically describing her marvelous experience while you are feeling nervous or perhaps ambivalent about having your baby, to say nothing of being physically uncomfortable. Even while you are being told about the happiness in store for you, you are bound to feel doubtful and apprehensive. Although the person characterizing her delivery as her most fulfilling experience is really trying to reassure you, wouldn't it be far better to be told the facts about what will happen rather than to hear an idealized version of this imminent and unexperienced event? Learning all you can protects you from feeling that something must be wrong with you if you do not entirely share your friends' enthusiasm."[1]

Be cautious while taking prepared childbirth instruction not to become so knowledgeable that there is no room for flexibility or change because you have already predetermined exactly how your delivery will proceed. You need to recognize that there are medical and psychological differences with each pregnancy. If you have a preprogrammed image of what your delivery is to be like, you or your spouse may be disappointed if things do not go exactly as you expect. There is no reason to be disappointed or to feel that you have failed as a mother or father. Many situations in a normal pregnancy cannot be foreseen. Prepared childbirth is designed to prepare you to meet those situations and also to help you to understand and be flexible enough to handle the unusual or the unexpected.

Dr. Salk says this about preparing for delivery:

"The best psychological preparation for delivery includes full knowledge of the delivery procedure, preparation in the form of exercises, training in breathing methods, and, most of all, in not setting up an idealized image of how you want your delivery to take place. If you decide in advance exactly how the delivery is going to occur, any medically necessary deviation from the anticipated pattern can only be viewed by you as a failure on your part. . . . Just prepare yourself for what is most likely to happen, though you also ought to know a little about unlikely events that could perhaps occur. Many people completely avoid coming to terms with the unexpected in advance because they don't want to make themselves anxious. Actually, knowing all you can might increase your anxiety somewhat, but your knowledge will prevent a feeling of failure from developing if your delivery requires some departure from the usual routine. . . .

"In your search for information and reassurance as your anxieties periodically surge, don't be surprised when you find people offering information that increases your anxiety rather than information that reduces it. . . . You will also notice that your feelings are being significantly influenced by past events. You may suddenly recall having heard your Aunt Mildred describe giving birth as an 'agony,' and you may remember that Aunt Mildred always described her 'horror' in hysterical terms. Although you were only ten at the time, as you now recollect her description your anxiety is sure to mount. You may even find it overwhelming, and you may quite properly seek reassurance from some authority. It's only normal to want to find some negation of Aunt Mildred's experience to alleviate your anxiety. Actually, I am convinced your rational reactions to anxiety caused by memories of Aunt Mildred's 'horror' is nature's way of making a mother vigilant and concerned about the birth of her child. To alleviate her anxiety, she seeks knowledge, and thus she is better prepared to deal with the normal and natural contingencies of childbirth."[2]

As the Due Date Approaches

As the time of delivery approaches, visits to the doctor for regular examinations will become more frequent. During the last month of pregnancy, the wife should see her doctor each week. The doctor will want to follow the progress of her pregnancy very carefully. He will be looking for any potential problems. He will want to make sure that both mother and baby are healthy.

The mother can help the doctor during the course of her pregnancy by making him aware of any problem she may be experiencing. Being pregnant brings about physical discomforts. Some of the discomforts are not normal and should be reported immediately. She should let the doctor know if she is experiencing any of the following symptoms during pregnancy: heartburn; excess gas; constipation; swelling—especially in the hands and feet; fainting; nausea; dizziness; headaches; fatigue; varicose veins; any form of cramps.

It is the doctor's responsibility to determine if these symptoms are important, not hers; but it is her responsibility to make him aware of any problems as soon as possible.

The doctor may also want to run some special tests for mother and baby.

One test that may be performed is the RH factor test. About 15 percent of people have what is known as RH negative blood type. The doctor will want to know ahead of time if her blood type is RH negative in order to prevent any problems. This blood type is not a problem with the first child because there are no antibodies in the mother's body to fight off the RH factor until after the birth of her first child. The doctor can take precautions so that any future children will not experience the ill effect of the RH negative factor.

Another blood test may be made to check for anemia, which is a lack of iron in the mother's blood. Anemia occurs because the baby's need for iron is increasing. If anemia is found, the doctor will supplement her diet with additional sources of iron.

A third test that is usually performed is the test for Rubella or German measles. Although measles is not serious for most people, it is extremely serious for unborn babies. The doctor will want to know immediately if the mother has been exposed to German measles, especially during the early stage of pregnancy. If she is not pregnant and has not had German measles, she should be tested for Rubella and be immunized before her first pregnancy. Be aware that her doctor will recommend a three-month waiting period after she receives immunization before she becomes pregnant.

Another test required in many states, the test for venereal disease, will be done at some point during the pregnancy.

These tests are necessary to ensure that your child will have a safe delivery and will be as healthy as possible at birth.

The doctor will also be watching the mother's weight very carefully, not because he is afraid she is eating too much, but because he is very interested in her health and the health of the baby. Pregnancy will be a lot harder on both of them if she is carrying excess weight. (Remember, it is easier to put pounds on than it is to take them off.) All women wonder how much weight they will gain. The weight gain will average between 20 and 27 pounds over the entire nine-month period, not nearly as much as some might think. That includes not only the weight of the baby, but also the weight of the placenta and the amniotic fluid, the increase in the size of the mother's breasts and of fat deposits on her abdomen that will serve to protect the baby and her own internal organs, and a general increase in body fluids. Let the doctor be your guide. Being pregnant is not the time to go on a diet.

When the due date is fast approaching, most mothers are ready for the baby to make its appearance; nine months is a long time to carry around that added weight. Many infants are born premature; that is, their delivery comes more than four weeks before their due date or they weigh less than five and one-half pounds. Having a premature infant is not a cause for major concern, because even infants weighing three to four pounds have a good chance of survival with today's medical technology. Premature birth, however, is still the largest cause of infant mortality in this country.

What happens when her due date has come and gone? Beside being disappointed, mother-to-be has now moved into a period of post-maturity—that is, delivery is two weeks or further beyond the due date. The greatest problem is the increase in size of the infant. Fortunately, God has created women with much elasticity and, normally, the post-mature baby causes few or no problems to the mother or infant.

The Beginning of Labor

The birth of a child is divided into three stages. The first stage is *labor*. The second stage is the actual *delivery of the baby*, and the third stage is the *delivery of the afterbirth* or the placenta.

WHAT DO YOU THINK?

1. What is labor?

2. List five signs that tell you labor is about to begin.
   (1)

   (2)

(3)

(4)

(5)

3. When are you to call the doctor once labor has begun?

4. What do you need to take to the hospital?

The most obvious sign that labor is about to begin is the due date approaching. Another sign is lightening, which normally occurs during the last few weeks of pregnancy. Lightening is the dropping of the baby's head into the pelvis in preparation for labor and delivery. There will be some noticeable changes in the mother's figure. Her waist will appear to drop and she will not feel so large. It should be easier for her to breathe because the pressure on the diaphragm will have diminished. She may need to urinate more frequently. She may also notice an exaggeration of the waddling that pregnant women experience.

The first stage of labor, childbirth, is divided into three phases; early labor, middle labor, and transition. It is important that both husband and wife understand each stage and each phase and know what the roles of husband and wife are to be during each stage of childbirth.

The First Stage—Labor

Early labor usually occurs before arriving at the hospital. During early labor, contractions are preceded or accompanied by a slight vaginal discharge of mucous or blood referred to as "the show." In most cases, labor follows within 48 hours of the show.

Also during early labor the amniotic sac or bag of water surrounding the unborn fetus ruptures. The rupture may appear as a slow leak or as a gush of water.

Once early labor has begun, it is important to follow as accurately as possible the childbirth method you have chosen. Stay home as long as possible in order to shorten the hospital stay. It will be necessary for you to begin using some of the techniques you learned in your childbirth class. Begin using the relaxation techniques taught by your childbirth instructor.

The cervical dilation will increase during early labor from 0 to 4 centimeters and the effacement of the cervix will be 100 percent by the time early labor is completed. Dilation is the opening of the cervix to permit the baby to be expelled from the uterus during delivery. For a baby to be born, the cervical opening must be 10 centimeters in diameter. So when the nurse comes in and says the mother is 4 centimeters dilated and 100 percent effaced, that means the cervix has thinned itself out as far as possible and opened to 4 centimeters in diameter. When this happens, the mother will be two-fifths of the way to delivery.

The father's role during early labor is to provide encouragement and reassurance to his wife. She will need to know that everything is okay. It is extremely important that the husband's attitude be one of confidence. During this time he will also keep a labor log or record of the frequency and length of contractions. During early labor, the contractions may be very erratic, occurring from 5 to 20 minutes apart and lasting from 30 to 60 seconds. Remember, every labor is different. It is very important to keep an accurate labor log. It is a picture of how often contractions are occurring and how long they last, and it indicates when to call the doctor and when to leave for the hospital.

Sometimes mothers experience "false" labor. There are several ways to determine whether the mother is in actual or false labor. During actual labor, contractions may be intensified by walking or changing activities; but during false labor, contractions may be relieved by moving around. During actual labor, contractions eventually become stronger, longer, and closer together. During false labor, contractions do not become longer or stronger. If the mother changes her activity and finds the pattern of her labor changing or contractions stopping, they are probably nothing but Braxton-Hicks contractions. She should sit down and relax or go back to sleep.

Generally speaking, a couple should call the doctor when labor begins. When labor contractions have lasted one hour and are between 5 and 10 minutes apart, it is time to call the doctor. One of the mistakes Rita and I made was not asking what the doctor meant by 5 minutes apart. Were we to call him the first time contractions were 5 minutes apart? Were we to average the number of contractions and then call him? Or were we to wait for a succession of contractions five minutes apart and then call him? This led to a great deal of confusion to the point that we waited for about 12 hours before calling the doctor because the contractions were irregular. Rita was not in any great discomfort at that point and the doctor would have told us to sit tight anyway, but nevertheless not knowing what to do was disconcerting.

After you have called the doctor and he has told you to go to the hospital, do so immediately. It would be to your benefit to have already made a practice trip to the hospital. It could be disconcerting once labor has begun, not to be able to find the parking lot or the admissions office or emergency entrance or not find the hospital itself! One caution for both expectant fathers and mothers: once labor has begun, mothers should refrain from eating or drinking anything other than clear fluids in order to prevent the possibility of vomiting during delivery.

WHAT DO YOU THINK?

1. After labor has begun and you and your spouse have arrived at the hospital, what is the first thing you expect to have to do?

2. Do you expect labor to be painful? If not, why not?

3. What is the husband's role during labor? List 10 things he should do during labor.

(1)

(2)

(3)

(4)

(5)

(6)

(7)

(8)

(9)

(10)

4. What role are you expecting God to play in your life and in the life of your spouse during labor and delivery? How will you know that He is actively involved?

When the expectant parents arrive at the hospital the first thing they should do is check in. If labor begins during the hospital's regular working hours, the couple will probably go to the admissions office. They may be required to fill out admission papers at that time if the mother has not been preadmitted. If labor begins outside of regular working hours, the couple will probably be directed to the emergency room entrance for admission.

Do you know where the admissions office is or where the emergency room entrance is? During what hours are you to use each?

After being admitted to the hospital, the mother will be taken to the maternity ward and into a labor room for preparation. The husband will probably be asked to leave the labor room during the time his wife is being "prepped"—changing into a hospital gown, shaving of the pubic area, being connected to an external-internal fetal monitor, and being given an enema. It is not necessary for the husband to leave the labor room while his wife is being prepped, it is only customary. The same custom usually applies during examinations while the mother is in labor. However, if during these times the wife needs her husband to fulfill his coaching role and provide support for her, there is nothing wrong with asking the hospital staff if her husband may be allowed to remain because she would like to have him present.

The degree of pain to be expected during labor depends on the mother's ability to relax and tolerate pain. It is not unusual for most women to be apprehensive about childbirth. This apprehension can grow quickly into fear—that is, fear of experiencing pain during labor. This fear really is a fear of the unknown. Natural or prepared childbirth is designed to reverse this process of fear, which causes tension, which in turn causes the muscles of the mother's body to remain firm or rigid and contracted. Fighting against contracting muscles causes pain, and pain produces new fears. Then the process begins again. It is easy to become trapped in a vicious circle. Through natural childbirth the couple learns to control the fears so that the mother can relax her muscles and thereby reduce the tension level and the degree of pain.

Throughout the course of labor, the mother will be examined by doctors and nurses to see how much progress she is making.

Remember, the average length of labor for the birth of a first child is approximately 16 hours. Remember also that it can be much shorter or much longer. There is no guarantee of how long labor will take.

During middle labor, the contractions come 2 to 5 minutes apart and last longer. They are perhaps 45 to 75 seconds in duration, and dilation of the cervix progresses from 4 to 8 centimeters. Effacement is completed. The mother's mood will become much more serious, and she will need to concentrate intensely to be able to relax.

During middle labor the mother may become increasingly tense or restless. Dilation will be progressing rapidly because of the strength of contraction. The baby will be moving down into the bony pelvis, toward the cervical opening.

There are several potential problems the father needs to be aware of. One may be that the baby's head is pressing against the mother's back causing back labor. It may be necessary for the father to use counter pressure or massage to alleviate this discomfort.

Another problem may be hyperventilation—the mother is breathing too fast or too deeply. It is important that the father slow down her breathing and make it more shallow. One way to do this is to have the mother breathe into a paper bag to alleviate the symptoms of hyperventilation.

Another problem is that the mother may lose her concentration, discovering she cannot follow her relaxation techniques. When this occurs it is important for the husband to assert himself, get his wife's full and complete attention, letting her know that he is there to help her.

The husband's role is to be sure that his wife is relaxed at all times. The more relaxed she becomes, the less tension she will experience, and consequently the pain will be diminished.

During Rita's labor with Nancy her ability to concentrate and practice the relaxation technique we had learned was so intense that she was not aware of other people walking into the room or asking her questions. The only voice she heard was mine. The husband must see that he is meeting his wife's needs and fulfilling her expectations during the course of labor.

The husband should give lots of encouragement, remembering

that each contraction is causing the cervix to efface further and to dilate. He should take any comforting measures to make labor easier for her—giving her back rubs; letting her suck ice chips—not liquids; rubbing a washcloth against her neck, face and arms. When her legs begin to shake, he can put a pair of socks on her or cover her legs with a blanket, keeping her comfortable but not overly-heated. The husband should remind his wife to empty her bladder every hour. A full bladder can stop the progress of labor and make contractions more difficult. One rule for both mother and father is to relax between contractions. The husband needs to be aware of any problems and take immediate steps to remedy them or notify the hospital staff.

Transition is the third phase of labor. During this time, cervical dilation will be completed, and dilation will reach 10 centimeters. The contractions will occur very close together and peak very quickly. They will last anywhere from 60 to 120 seconds or longer with three or four peaks. During transition, the contractions are the longest and strongest. Transition is the most intense phase of labor but it is also the shortest.

Because of the intensity of contractions, the mother in transition may experience a myriad of feelings. She may become irritable, angry, moody, discouraged, or may even want to yell at her husband during this phase of labor. Or she may want to go to sleep. It is not unusual for her not to want to have the baby. Her senses may be sharper; she may have stomach problems; she may have the chills or the sweats; she may want to chase her husband out of the room. All these things are very normal. The husband is very much needed at this time and it is important for both husband and wife to focus on the positive aspect of the transition phase—that the baby will be born very soon.

Touch may be a very important factor in communicating relaxation to the mother during this phase. She may not want to be touched at all, but her husband should not become discouraged with her irritability. It may not be possible for the husband to meet all of his wife's needs at this time. He cannot make her unpregnant; he cannot stop the process of labor; he cannot control the length or speed of contractions. He can, however, continue to remain confident and reassure her whenever necessary. One thing that helped during the process of our labor when things became difficult was the opportunity to pray for each other. God has provided a special bond between members of the Body of Christ through His Spirit. This is a time when prayer can help provide emotional support to a member of the Body who may be discouraged.

If the mother has an urge to push or feels she is about to have a bowel movement, or if she begins to hold her breath and bear down, call the nurse immediately. The husband must be very firm because transition is not the time to push. The pushing needs to come during the delivery itself.

The Second Stage—Delivery of the Baby

During the second stage of childbirth—delivery—dilation will be complete, the baby will be moving down through the birth canal, and the vaginal tissues will be unfolding. Contractions will occur 2 to 4 minutes apart and will last about 60 seconds or longer. They usually appear to be milder than contractions during transition. When the mother is prepared for the second stage of childbirth, she will be taken to the delivery room and her husband will put on his hospital greens, his sterile covering. The mother will be given instruction to begin pushing, pushing the baby out into the world.

Once she is told to push, the mother will feel a great deal of relief. She may experience some burning sensations around the perineum because the baby's head will be stretching the perineum. The doctor may perform an episiotomy or a small cut to keep the birth canal from tearing. A clean incision heals much more rapidly than a rip or a tear.

If the doctor says that crowning has appeared—that the baby's head can be seen at the opening of the vagina—the husband will need to provide good support for his wife so that she can use all of her energy to push. He will help hold her up and will need to remind her to relax her muscles. The more relaxed she becomes, the more efficient her contractions will be.

As soon as delivery is complete, the new baby will be wiped off. Normally the doctor will use a rubber suction bulb to clear the breathing passages of the baby; he will clamp and cut the umbilical cord and hand the baby over to the pediatrician for care.

The pediatrician will probably mention an Apgar rating (score) in the delivery room. This simple test is done at one minute and repeated again five minutes after birth to rate five different aspects of the newborn. Each aspect receives 0, 1, or 2 points. The five areas that are scored are the (1) respiratory efforts—ability of the baby to cry, (2) muscle tone, (3) reflexes, (4) infant's color, and (5) heart rate. The highest score possible is 10 at both intervals. Very few doctors score any baby at 10. The 5-minute score is the more accurate prediction of the baby's normality and ability to survive. Most babies score a six and nine, which means that everything improved from the 1-minute to the 5-minute score.

Silver nitrate, required by law in most states, will be applied to the infant's eyes to prevent eye infection. The baby's footprints are taken in the delivery room and probably a fingerprint of the mother to prevent an accidental mixup of babies. In most cases the doctor will allow the new mother and father to hold their baby, and for the first time they will get to meet God's special gift to them.

Delivery of the Afterbirth—the Third Stage

The third stage of labor is the expulsion of the placenta. Even after your child is delivered, the mother will continue to experience mild contractions, which force the placenta free from the uterus and push it down the vagina so it can be expelled. Your doctor will inspect the uterus to make sure everything has been expelled. The mother may be given a shot to shrink the uterus, and if an episiotomy was performed, the doctor will suture the mother and prepare her for the recovery room where she will be monitored closely for a period of time. The baby will be moved to a nursery where its status will also be monitored for the next few hours.

WHAT'S YOUR PLAN?

1. List five questions you would like to ask before the birth of your baby.

(1)

(2)

(3)

(4)

(5)

2. What will you take to the hospital? List at least 10 things you will need during labor and 10 things Mom will need during her hospital stay.

	During Labor	In the Hospital
(1)		
(2)		
(3)		
(4)		
(5)		
(6)		
(7)		
(8)		

(9)

(10)

3. Name two emotional needs you have or think you might have about labor and delivery. Share these needs with your spouse.

4. For the husband: Develop a plan to meet your wife's needs during labor and delivery. Make your plan specific. How will she know you are sharing her burdens?

Notes

All material quoted is used by permission.
1. Lee Salk, *Preparing for Parenthood* (New York: Bantam Books, 1974), pp. 69,70.
2. *Ibid.*, pp. 70-73.

What Price Baby?

Returning home from one of the frequent shopping trips necessary to prepare for the coming of a new arrival, one wife proudly
announced, "I just bought something our new baby can't do
without. It's supposed to quiet an infant down in 30 seconds or put
him to sleep in 60 seconds." What might this marvel of modern
technology be? Would you believe a teddy bear, complete with
intrauterine sounds similar to the ones the infant heard during its
nine months of development? An enterprising doctor had placed a
microphone inside the uterus of an expectant mother, close to the
infant's ear, recorded the sound and duplicated the sound on tapes.
The tapes were put inside the teddy bears designed to lull the infant
population of America to sleep.

Sound farfetched? Well, it's true. This is just one of the many
products on the market that compete for the dollars of new parents.
This is a far cry from the humble birth of our Lord who, after His
arrival in a stable, was wrapped in swaddling clothes and laid in a
manger. Joseph's expenses were quite minimal, perhaps the cost of
the night's lodging and maybe the services of a midwife (although
this isn't recorded in the Scripture).

How much does it cost to have a child today?

WHAT DO YOU THINK?

1. What is the cost of a normal hospital delivery in your area?

2. What does the doctor's fee run? What does it include?

3. With your spouse, make a list of everything the baby will need at home (furniture, clothes, supplies, linens, etc.).

4. How much will these items cost?

5. List three resources you have at your disposal to pay for a child.

(1)

(2)

(3)

Financial responsibility is a key to providing a secure future for any family. In these inflation-prone times the cost of having a child and raising a child are on the increase. Rising hospital and medical fees have increased so dramatically in the late 1970s that the costs involved in giving birth to a child can rival the purchase of a new car. This is not being said to give the impression that a car is as important as a child, but merely to demonstrate that God's people need to practice good stewardship, sound planning. A child should be seen as a gift from God that will grow in value, not as a financial drain where the road to the poorhouse is compared with Pampers.

Doctor's Fees

Inflationary costs and the need for sound planning were made abundantly clear when Rita and I found out we were expecting our second child. Our first child was delivered by cesarean birth in the fall of 1978. Our obstetrician's fee was $950. If you think that was high then sit down and get out the smelling salts, because our next one will weigh in at $1,400. Before you have a heart attack, vote for socialized medicine, or decide not to have children, consider what the fee includes and what other professionals in your community earn. Considering the amount of care provided and a fair estimate of the doctor's time, his remuneration is seen more realistically as something less than $70 per hour, much less than other medical specialists receive and less than attorneys and other professionals in our community receive. Dr. Robert E. Hall had the following to say about doctors' fees:

"*Average Fees.* It is impossible to generalize on this tender subject, for fees vary somewhat from patient to patient, from doctor to doctor, and from community to community. Most obstetricians charge a flat rate for their service, which includes antepartum care, labor, delivery, and hospital care, and at least one postpartum visit. Ask the doctor on your first visit not only what his fee will be, but also what it includes. There are, of course, a few unpredictable extras for which additional charges are sometimes made—such as the performance of a cesarean section or circumcision—but routine procedures such as forceps deliveries and episiotomies are almost invariably covered.

"The barest minimum for this nine-month care by a specialist is $250. Fees are higher than this in the bigger cities and, of course, doctors traditionally tend to adjust their fees somewhat to the patient's ability to pay.

"*What You're Buying.* When you pay your obstetrician you are buying many intangibles: his training, his experience, his availability, his patience, his confidence, his knowledge, and his time. Calculated in more understandable terms, let us say that you see your doctor ten times before the delivery, he spends six hours in the labor suite with you, he sees you five times in the hospital and once again in his office six weeks later. If he charges you $250 for this work, he is being remunerated at a rate of about $25 an hour—a pretty low rate for a professional man. Few specialists in other fields would settle for that, let alone a television repairman. And this calculation does not include the phone calls, the lost sleep, the delayed meals, and the time involved in getting to and from the hospital. You may see your doctor only five times and your labor may take only two hours, while your neighbor may see him twenty times and be in labor for two days; it wouldn't be fair to charge her a bigger fee, any more than it would be fair to charge a fat man more for his suits."[1]

Your doctor normally will require payment by the end of the seventh month unless other arrangements have been made in advance.

Hospital Charges

Hospital costs vary widely. A home birth could cost only a few hundred dollars, while the seven-day average stay for a cesarean birth could run several thousand dollars. You will be billed for nearly everything you or your child use or consume during your hospital stay. Room, IVs, medications, and special procedures all will appear on your final bill. There will be charges for labor room, delivery room, hospital room, and nursery. Even charges for the assistant doctor, anesthesiologist, pediatrician, and nurse will appear on your bill.

As you can see by now, even the most normal pregnancy can cost from $1,000 to $2,500 and move up from there. Being surprised by a $5,000 hospital bill with no way to meet it is not an example of good planning. God's people have a responsiblity to plan in order to know what God wants us to do and to be (see Col. 3:10). Good planning now, before having children, can save you money, time, and frustration.

How will you pay for your child? There are many possibilities available to you.

Regular income: A fortunate few have no financial problems because their income is sufficient to meet the expenses incurred by having a child.

Savings: If your plan is to save, anticipate inflation and keep track of current fees in order to adjust your plans.

Loans: A viable possibility when no other exists.

Relatives: Family members can help, but only if there are no strings attached to the offer. In our counseling ministry it is not unusual to find well-meaning parents who have taken over financial responsibility as well as physical responsibility for the new baby; consequently the new parents feel that their role has been usurped. Grandparents could better help by giving financial gifts of a general nature rather than by saying, "We're paying for our new grandchild." The more that parents, relatives, and friends can do to help the new parents see the child as their own, the smoother the transition to parenthood will be. "Honor one another above yourselves" (Rom. 12:10, *NIV*). Honor the new parents and their new role.

Insurance: Good medical coverage can protect you from catastrophic financial problems. One problem that often occurs is an attitude that "it won't happen to me." Unfortunately, insurance agents won't come knocking on your door to pay your expenses after you have become sick; nor can you apply for medical coverage to pay for a pregnancy already underway. Rita and I have had medical insurance since before our marriage. During the first 10 years of our marriage, our medical expenses amounted to only a fraction of what we were paying in premiums. Insurance seemed a waste to us at the time because it would have been cheaper to pay medical costs as they were incurred and skip the monthly premiums. However, with a major illness, loss of a baby, Nancy's birth, and the expectation of another birth, that has changed. Our insurance premiums are now cheap at twice the cost.

If you do not have medical coverage it would be wise to consult an insurance agent to find out what coverage is available. Check with your employer to see if a group policy is available. If you have insurance and decide to change jobs during a pregnancy, will you still be covered under your old policy? Will you have to pay your doctor's fees and then wait for reimbursement from the insurance company after your child's birth? We would like to share a word of encouragement with you. Our cesarean birth was not planned and not even considered until Rita was in her thirtieth hour of labor. We were not thinking of cost at that point but we were greatly comforted when our $5,000 bill cost us only $400. Our insurance covered the balance, and we are very thankful for our planning.

Other resources are available to you that you may not be aware of. In many states disability payments are available to a working woman. Hospital payments are available in some states (for example, in 1979 California was paying $12 per day during hospitalization). This payment is made directly to the individual, but it must be applied for. Pregnancy is now treated as an illness under a 1979 federal law. Therefore, you may be entitled to sick leave benefits from your employer if you had sick leave coming for any other illness.

Housing

If you find it necessary to move because your current house or apartment is too small, too expensive, or doesn't allow children, then moving is another expense that must be included in your budget.

WHAT DO YOU THINK?

1. Where will your new family live?

2. Is your present home or apartment large enough?

3. Are children allowed where you currently live?

4. Is where you are living now where you want your child to grow up?

5. List any changes you will need to make in your housing situation.

6. List any remodeling or redecorating you will need to do for your new child. Is your home safe for a new baby?

Take a moment to close your eyes. Imagine you are walking into your baby's room. What will you see first? What color is the room? How is it decorated?

Who will do your decorating—yourself, a professional, or others? Will you paint or wallpaper? Both can be lovely. Do you want to match your colors to the sex of your child? If you do, you can order items well ahead of time to be delivered when you call the store from the hospital.

You can save yourself money by taking your time in shopping; the prices of infant furnishings vary widely depending on where you shop. By planning early, you can take advantage of sales, discount stores, and gifts. When friends and relatives ask what they can get the new baby, have a list of your needs. Friends often will commit themselves to specific items or are willing to contribute to a large item you really want. A gift of diaper service can greatly reduce that $25-a-month expense after the birth of your child. Many of the items you really need could end up as special gifts from dear friends if they know what you want. Don't be afraid to let people know your needs; people are much more willing to give you something if they know it is really your desire.

While we are talking about friends and gifts, two items to purchase early are a gift record and thank-you notes. Thank the people God has moved to meet your needs. They deserve your courtesy, care, and concern.

Other ways to save money on the birth of your first child can include: using hand-me-downs from friends and relatives (furniture, clothing, and supplies); searching garage sales and second-hand stores; purchasing items from unfinished furniture stores; borrowing things from friends who have not completed their families but who aren't using the crib, playpen, etc., at this time.

Nursery Furniture and Supplies

The crib: Naturally the crib is essential; the baby will sleep in it for the first two to four years of his life. In fact, a full-size crib—one that measures 54 by 30 inches—is considered a "six-year size," though in my experience almost every child graduates to a bed by the time he is four. You can also find a smaller crib—to fit into a smaller nursery—which has the advantage of rolling easily through doorways if you think you will be bringing your baby up with nomadic sleeping patterns. And some cribs convert later into youth beds, saving you an extra expense in the future.

Nearly all cribs today are carefully made so that the bars are no more than 3¼ inches apart to prevent baby's head from getting caught between them when he peeks out. They have an easily locked, deep drop side that makes it easier to get to the baby yet will keep him from falling out. Check to see that your selection has these features. A crib that allows you to adjust the mattress height is also convenient, as are casters which make it easy to move the crib about. Look for strong construction (hard, durable finish, and a minimum—if any—of external hardware). A plastic-coated dropside rail will keep a teething baby from eating the finish. Shop the nursery furniture stores near you; the salespeople are generally very helpful about explaining the good points of various styles and helping you decide which is right for you. If you will be painting a hand-me-down crib, make sure your paint is lead free.

The crib is the first item to sketch into your room plan because it should be in the light, airy part of the room but not in direct, brilliant sunlight or in drafts and not within reach of dangerously grabbable things such as light cords, venetian blind cords, and hanging pictures. Once you have found the perfect place for the crib, the other items will take their places in relation to it.

Give as much thought to the purchase of your crib mattress as you do to the crib itself. It should be resilient yet firm to start your baby on his way to healthy posture. Get the best you can; it is an important investment.

All other pieces of nursery furniture should be chosen carefully too. God is giving you a gift whose care, upbringing, nurturing, physical existence, and spiritual development are given over to you who receive this precious gift. Inspect all items for safety—this is concern number one: no sharp corners, no protruding points, and no parts that could pinch small fingers or poke inquisitive eyes.

Another matter of safety not to be overlooked is the possibility of lead-based paints having been used on furniture or walls in the past. If you have any doubt about painted surfaces, remove the old paint, seal and refinish with two coats of non-toxic, lead-free paint. Or move!

Marcia Morton's *Pregnancy Notebook* gives a detailed discussion of each item of furniture you may need.[2]

Diapers: Many women prefer, and have time to launder, their own diapers. In order to do this properly, you will need an initial purchase of between three and four dozen diapers. Your pediatrician can recommend special products to soak out bacteria that can cause diaper rashes. Use caution at all times when it comes to anything that will come in contact with baby's fine skin. Even the commercial softeners that you use for your own clothes can contain perfumes that may cause the infant's skin to react.

One way around the constant chore of laundering diapers is to use disposables. Their cost is comparable to diaper service, about $300 per year.

The cheapest and easiest way to go in our opinion is a commercial diaper service which will provide about 100 clean diapers each week. They are delivered and picked up at your door. Although the cost may seem high, the only time you spend is in bagging last week's used diapers, and you don't have to make trips to and from the store.

Linens: A good supply of linens for the crib, bassinet, bath, and carriage is always necessary. You will be surprised how quickly they become soiled by an infant.

Clothing: A checklist of clothing is provided for your convenience in the "What's Your Plan?" section of this chapter. It lists the infant's basic needs during its first year. When choosing clothing, remember to pick items that wash easily, provide growing room, are comfortable, and are convenient to get into and out of. Don't buy too much; infants outgrow their clothing quickly.

Special Items of Interest

Birth announcements: Choose birth announcements ahead of

time and call the printer from the hospital. Friends and relatives will want to hear from you as soon as possible. Rita had prepared a name and address list before she went to the hospital and was able to use the week's stay to get most of our announcements mailed before she left the hospital.

Flowers: Congratulatory bouquets are exciting to receive. One of our roles is to "build one another up," and flowers sent to your wife may help her feel special at a time when the newborn is getting all the attention.

Older children often have a hard time understanding why the baby is getting all the attention. They may be feeling very lonely. One of the things Rita and I do when a friend has a new baby and we are delivering a gift for the infant is to take along a small, wrapped gift for each of the other children in the family to let them know we are thinking about them too. Rita is planning to have a number of gifts wrapped before she enters the hospital for the birth of our next child which we can give to Nancy at the time of our new baby's birth. We want our children to love each other and not feel that they have to compete for attention.

Photographs: An excellent investment for parents to make in the life of their child is photographs. When child rearing is over, you have the end product—a man or woman of God's creation through an act of love—but memories are so much clearer with a photographic record of your child's progress and history.

Parents' sanity fund: We set aside money for baby-sitting. It allows us freedom to be married to each other, not to an infant. It allows nights out together and freedom for Rita to do things on her own too.

WHAT'S YOUR PLAN?

Developing a practical budget will greatly help you understand and prepare to meet the cost involved in having a child of your own. In order to help you develop your budget, the following worksheets will guide you in planning and keeping records of needs, supplies, medical care, and actual costs. With your spouse, fill in the estimated cost column. Keep your record handy and up to date. Take it with you when shopping, and record actual costs beforehand whenever possible. The worksheet is designed as a handy checklist to facilitate more complete planning. Check each item when completed.

	Estimated Cost	Actual Cost	Date Needed	Date Acquired	Tax Deductions
Medical Care					
Obstetrician					
Pediatrician					
Hospital					
First year					
Dentist					
Baby nurse					
Hospital					
Labor room					
Delivery room					
Hospital room					
Nursery fee					
Anesthesia					
Assisting physician					
Anesthesiologist					
Miscellaneous					
Circumcision					
Supplies					
Total	_____	_____			
Less Insurance	_____	_____			
Our cost	_____	_____			

Nursery Needs
Layette
Crib
Mattress
Chest of drawers
Lamp
Decorations
Dressing table
Reclining infant seat
Vaporizer

Bumper pads
Car seat

Clothing
    Baby
    Booties (3,4 sets)
    Gowns (4,5)
    Shirts (4-6)
    Plastic pants (5)
    Sleeping sacks (3)
    Sweaters (2)
    Hats (2)
    Bibs (4)
    Stretchable sleepers (4-6)
    Receiving blankets (5)

    Mom
    Maternity wardrobe

      Total   _____   _____
      Less Gifts   _____   _____
      Our cost   _____   _____

Supplies
Baby soap
Baby lotion
Baby oil
Baby shampoo
Baby powder
Disposable baby wipes
Something for diaper rash
Cotton balls and swabs
Rectal thermometer
Petroleum jelly
Bath tub/bathinet
Large bath towels (4)
Sponge bath pillow
Wash cloths

Comb and brush
Fingernail scissors

Bedding
Crib sheets (4-6)
Crib blankets (2)
Waterproof pads (2)

Feeding
Disposable nurser kit or four 4-ounce and eight 8-ounce bottles and
    sterilizer
Extra nipples for bottles
Nipple brush and nursing pads
Nipple shields and breast pump
Breast cream
Feeding dish, spoon, and bibs

Diapering
Diaper service (80 to 100 per week)
Home laundered (3 to 4 dozen)
Disposable diapers for travel
Diaper pins (4-6)
Diaper liners
Diaper pail
Diaper bag

Total cost	_____	_____
Less Gifts	_____	_____
Our cost	_____	_____

Total of all "our costs":   _____

Notes

All material quoted is used by permission.
1. Robert E. Hall, *Nine Months' Reading* (New York: Bantam Books, 1977), pp. 9,10.
2. Marcia C. Morton, *Pregnancy Notebook* (New York: Bantam Books, Inc., 1972), pp. 49-64.

Baby Has Arrived—
Now What?

What will it be like to be a parent? You have ideas, expectations, and dreams now, but being a parent may be different than you anticipate. Many parents feel differently after the baby arrives than they did prior to birth.

How do you visualize your baby? A peaceful, responsive, plump quiet baby nesting in your arms? Few parents visualize a tense, wiry, screaming, hyperactive baby, but this is what many parents end up with. Your feelings will be influenced by your baby's looks, temperament, behavior, smiles, and any other characteristics. You need to be honest with yourself about all of your feelings, including the negative ones. Accept your feelings and voice them.

Some days you might wonder why you wanted a child. "What was I thinking of to get myself tied down in this way?" You probably had ambivalent feelings about pregnancy, and you will have the same feelings as a new parent. The more negative a mother feels about having a baby, the greater is the possibility of physiological and psychological reaction. You will get over these ambivalent feelings if you admit them; all parents experience these feelings. Who really enjoys changing diaper after diaper?

Your feelings are important, because how you feel before and after its birth will help determine how you relate to the child later on. Your feelings will affect your child more than your principles and techniques of child rearing and they will change because of constantly changing developmental needs.

Don't be too surprised at how you feel and behave in your early stages as a parent. Your behavior at this time will probably be consistent with your behavior in other areas of your life. When your child is born, you will be called on to be flexible and shift from one behavior to another as your child changes. [1]

Adjustments for Mother

Don't try to be a super mother. There is no such creature. If you think you must be the perfect mother you are setting yourself up to feel inadequate. Many mothers learn to despise themselves because they fail to be perfect. Soon they fall into depression.

For many years you have carried with you a "fantasy mother" image. This "fantasy" was created from movies, television, magazines, how-to books, novels, and even friends, and the fantasy is probably that of a super mother. Two common fantasies are "the house should always be immaculate" and "I should always look great." Are these fantasies realistic? If an immaculate house or looking good is so important to you, what can be done about it?

WHAT DO YOU THINK?

1. Describe the kind of mother you imagine you will be (your wife will be). Which parts of the description are realistic and which are not?

2. What are some specific, realistic goals that you would like to reach as a mother (to see your wife attain after the birth of the child)?

    a.

    b.

c.

d.

e.

3. Describe the plan you will develop to attain these goals.

One of the fears a mother may experience is that she will be incompetent in caring for her new baby. This fear is normal. Just because one is a woman doesn't mean that motherhood is instinctive. Get rid of the belief that you have to perform perfectly right away. Every mother feels inept, no matter how much preparation she has had. A woman's feelings of motherhood may not be strong at first; they may have to grow. Our society has portrayed mothers as automatically loving and gushing over their baby. Motherhood (and fatherhood to some degree) has been likened to prearranged marriages—you do not meet until you see each other after your roles have already been arranged. Now mother and baby are stuck with each other. There is no slow way to ease into this relationship.

Some mothers may think that her role is one of always giving. Give, give, give, and no let-up in sight. "Good mothers always do for their children, are always available, never leave them, and put their own needs last" is the way the routine goes. But how can she give to another when she has nothing left to give? A mother needs to be sure she gets the following:

● uninterrupted rest
● good food (our body is a temple of the Holy Spirit and needs attention)
● time alone to care for herself (like a bubble bath or a trip to the beauty parlor)
● time with other supportive adults
● exercise, shopping, or whatever is pleasurable.

A mother needs to evaluate her schedule and tasks in terms of available time and energy. In addition to all of her previous household tasks, she now has a new baby to care for. Maybe she used to spend two or three hours preparing each meal; simple meals may be in order. After her baby is born she may find herself cleaning once a week instead of three times a week. Becoming a slave to the home or a baby is not necessary. Most mothers find they need to give up some things and alter their previous schedule. However, although some activities on the mother's schedule may not be essential, they should not be eliminated because they are necessary for her own development. Cooking a favorite dessert that takes extra time, gardening, going to the exercise class—all are examples of activities that perhaps should not be cut if they provide her with joy and fulfillment.

WHAT DO YOU THINK?

1. List four to eight activities which you feel you (or your wife) may have to alter or drop after your baby is born.

2. List four to eight activities which you feel your husband (or you) may have to alter or drop after your baby is born.

3. Share your lists and discuss the changes you may have to make in your schedules.

Adjustments for Father

The father's postpartum adjustment can be similar to the mother's. Some of the same problems are present, although the father is away from home during much of the day. What do you think are some of the biggest adjustments or problems a father faces?

Often a new father struggles with the feeling that he gets whatever time, attention, and affection are left over. He feels displaced. Fathers do get leftovers because the baby gets the prime time and attention. Fathers can handle this problem best if they accept it before the baby is born. The loss of freedom because of family responsibilities can cause resentment if not accepted early.

Spontaneity and freedom change after the baby is born; quality time for each other may now have to be planned. A new mother often finds that she is exhausted by the time her husband gets home from work. Maybe she needs a nap beforehand, or together when he arrives home. Private time together each day and a date together each week will do wonders for both. A baby has the potential to strain a marital relationship, but strain need not occur. It will, however, if you let it.

Sometimes the father must adjust to the gender of the baby—he wanted a boy and got a girl. If the first child is not a male, the father may want more children for the specific purpose of having a boy. A father-to-be can analyze his reasons for preference and anticipate his feelings if he is disappointed. Many marriages experience a strain because of the father's disappointment.

Somtimes a father is not prepared for parenting. If he has learned about caring for the baby—feeding, bathing, changing and comforting—before it arrives he will feel more confident. Learning about child care through classes and experience with other children is very important.

Remember, the baby belongs to both father and mother. A baby is to be cared for, loved, and fondled by the father as well as the mother. So-called "mothering" chores or roles *can* give a father satisfaction. Sharing child-care responsibilities also helps the marital relationship grow closer.

A father does not need correction from the mother: "No, that's not the way to hold the baby," "Don't feed her so fast; I've told you that before." Such correction is one of the most frequent and rift-creating mistakes that occur early in parenting. Some mothers have pushed the father away from child care by over protection and continual criticism and then complained about the father's lack of involvement. If a husband doesn't know exactly what to do, constructive sharing will help. Use positive encouragement but not criticism. Ephesians 4:15 and Romans 14:13 convey the pattern to use at this time: "Speaking the truth in love . . . " and, "Stop being so critical of one another." A father may do the task differently from the mother but that doesn't mean his way is wrong.

Division of household tasks and roles is another major area of adjustment. An unplanned arrangement has the potential for resentment and stress and feelings of exclusion. Couples who have worked out tasks together (according to abilities and time, not stereotyped male-female roles) avoid the father-involved-outside-the-home and mother-does-all-at-home syndrome. Some couples prefer the traditional pattern rather than sharing tasks within the home. The important thing is that both agree on the division of responsibilities.

Some husbands have arranged with their place of employment a flexible schedule so they are able to arrive home earlier to assist their wives. Not all employers may agree to such a schedule, but it is worth asking about.

Family support and encouragement can assist both the new mother and new father. It takes away the feeling of being all alone.[2]

WHAT DO YOU THINK?

1. Describe the kind of father you imagine you will be (your husband will be). Which parts of the description are realistic and which are not?

2. What are some specific, realistic goals that you would like to reach as a father (to see your husband attain) after the birth of the child ?

    a.

    b.

c.

d.

e.

3. Describe the plan you will develop to attain these goals.

Emotional Responses Following Birth

Depression is a very common experience mothers suffer following childbirth. This type of, or occasion for, depression is often misunderstood. It is commonly called the "four-day blues" or "postpartum depression." It occurs in the mother who has recently given birth to a baby.

Many mothers have what is popularly called "postpartum blues," a period of mild depression following delivery that usually lasts only a few days. It is a condition that makes more than 50 percent of women miserable and about five percent of them seriously so. Thus it deserves careful consideration.

It is often difficult to identify the cause of postpartum blues, if indeed there is one cause, because many of the physiological and psychological changes that occur are a result of pregnancy, labor, and delivery. No mother gives birth without experiencing some form of stress. The stress may be physical—with obvious pain, fatigue, and sudden hormonal changes. Today the various drugs given to patients in labor may cause a side effect that produces changes in the women's mental state.

Emotional stress is also invariably present. Few women enter labor without some degree of fear and anxiety. They may have fear of pain, injury or death. Or they may be anxious about the child: Will it be normal, will it live, how will I cope on my own? These and many other anxieties are common to most pregnant women.

In theory, the woman who gives birth to a live, healthy child is expected to feel pride and satisfaction, but this is not always so. The mother who does not feel overjoyed may consider herself a failure or an abnormal person lacking in maternal feeling and normal emotions.

Sometimes a mother's emotional turmoil is the result of physical change. During pregnancy, physiological changes such as estrogen and progesterone production increase dramatically. But after delivery, levels of these hormones suddenly drop, much like the change that occurs at the beginning of the menstrual period, only far more pronounced. The body, however, has a way of compensating for such abrupt changes. Simultaneous with the drop in estrogen and progesterone there is a rise in the level of prolactin, a pituitary hormone responsible for the secretion of milk from the breast and for stimulating what doctors have come to recognize as maternal or nurturing, instincts.

Emotionally, too, there is a letdown after delivery. Labor is an intense emotional event culminating in delivery, and after carrying a child for nine months, the mother sometimes feels that this is only the beginning. She realizes that not only has she produced a new individual but she will be responsible for him for a long time.

An additional reason for a letdown on the part of the mother is lack of attention. During the nine months of pregnancy she has been the center of attention. People have been concerned about her and have talked about her and the upcoming birth of the baby. She has been given special courtesies, extra attention, gifts, and then all of a sudden she is no longer the center of attention. Now the attention is given to the baby. This is a difficult adjustment for some mothers.

The new mother may face environmental stresses as well. She may never have been in a hospital before and the routine is unfamiliar. The nurses are strangers, busy with their own tasks. In some hospitals the baby is kept in the nursery rather than in the mother's room, and she can't see or hold him whenever she wants. When he is brought to her, he may be sleepy and unresponsive or even crying. If she tries to nurse, the milk may not come at first or her nipples may hurt. Sometimes her stitches are uncomfortable or she has afterbirth pains.

The new mother may also be unsure of herself in her new role; hence, too many helpful suggestions and words of advice may cause her to become tense and upset. She may worry about obtaining the approval of her neighbor or her mother, and she may resent their advice.

When a baby has come into the family, the woman finds that she is no longer just a woman and wife. She has become woman, wife, and mother, which requires a change in her self-concept. Before the baby was born she may have seen herself as a school girl, bride, or career girl. Some of these roles now may seem incompatible with her new role as mother; hence, conflict may arise. She may find it difficult to give up her career and although many women continue to work after the baby is born, adequate arrangements must be made for his care.

The mother and father can no longer do things on the spur of the moment since an evening out will mean that they must arrange for a baby-sitter. This adjustment can be difficult for the new mother or for the mother whose other children are older and have become more independent. She must give up part of her former role identity and establish a new role in which she can be happy. The mother can still be a creative person who works in the community, but she will have to consider the infant as she plans for her own self-fulfillment.

One author described four different yet common syndromes among young mothers:

"Pools-Winner" syndrome. This syndrome seems to occur in women who have been trying to become pregnant for some time without success and who then suddenly find they have hit the jackpot. They go through pregnancy in a state of mild euphoria and then, when the child arrives, they collapse into a state of acute anxiety and depression. This situation seems baffling to those who knew how much the child was wanted. Indeed, the mother frequently says, "Why should I feel like this? Now I have everything I want!" This statement is the clue to the problem. The anxiety is

caused by a fear of losing that which she wanted so badly.

"Playing house" syndrome. Some women marry at an early age before they have really developed the capacity for a full, adult relationship. Their motives for doing so are varied, but often marriage is seen as a way of escaping from home. Such wives may be relatively inexperienced and lack knowledge in sexual matters and so find themselves pregnant before they have had an opportunity to develop their feminine role. Faced with the reality of a child, a husband, and a home, they may well decide that this particular game is not for them after all; so they consider returning to their parents' home so that mother can take over the baby.

"Immaculate conception" syndrome. Most of us know a woman whose house is more of a shrine than a home—a place where dust sheets cover the rugs that cover the carpets, and even the front lawn is polished. Such a person with rigid, perfectionistic ideas may have great difficulty adjusting to the arrival of a noisy, dirty, and demanding child. She wants to see herself as the perfect mother with the perfect child and finds it difficult to tolerate shortcomings in herself or the child.

"Praying mantis" syndrome. The female praying mantis has the charming habit of devouring the male as he completes the act of copulation. Few women treat their husbands in this way but some tend to behave toward them as if, having fathered a child, their usefulness is at an end. The husband is ignored and his needs are neglected for those of the child. Sexual relationships may not be resumed, and the wife uses the 365 well-known excuses. A variant of this game is the "martyrdom syndrome" in which the wife suffers, or believes she suffers, some damage during childbirth. She may then take the attitude that her husband, being responsible for this happening, must be made to suffer in turn. "How could you have done it to me, you brute?" is her theme song. This is often followed by, "Don't forget what the doctor said."

Although postpartum blues usually occur three or four days after delivery, a similar reaction may occur two, three, or even four weeks after the mother is home. Such upsets are often triggered by stresses that have been building up since the baby arrived. For instance, the husband may feel ignored because the infant takes up so much of his wife's time and affection. Well-meaning relatives and friends may have begun to drop over more frequently, requiring additional housework and preparation.

Conquering Postpartum Blues

Whatever the cause of late postpartum blues, their occurrence is a signal for both husband and wife to reevaluate their life-style and consider ways to improve the situation.

Whether the "blues" occur three days or three weeks after the baby arrives, they usually disappear without permanent ill effects. If they last longer than one or two weeks, you should go for help.[3]

What can a husband do if his wife becomes depressed and especially if the depression continues?

Understanding the causes and symptoms of depression is the first step toward helping. If your wife is so depressed that she just stares or ignores greetings and turns away from you, remember that she doesn't want to act this way. In severe depression, the person loses his ability to govern his thinking and emotions. If you understand how your wife is feeling and why she is acting the way she is, if you understand that her behavior is the normal behavior of a depressed person, then you can be in better control of your own responses.

If the depression continues for several weeks, take your wife to a doctor. Your family physician may be able to help or may recommend someone. The time factor is very important. Don't let depression go on and on. Even if she keeps putting you off and refusing to go, make the arrangements, find someone to watch the baby, guide her firmly into the car, and go! As long as you tolerate the other's depression, you are helping to maintain it.

Give your wife your full support. Make other close family members aware of the situation and give them instructions on how to respond. Confrontations with a depressed person should be avoided. Tell others not to attack the depressed person, not to bring up failures, not to be harsh, and not to ask her to do things that she is not capable of doing while depressed.

Don't avoid your wife when she is depressed. Avoiding her will further isolate her and could make her worse. You might want to avoid her because you experience guilt over her depression, thinking that you may be the cause. Positive loving comments and compliments are important; so is physical contact.

Understand that when your wife is depressed, she really hurts. Don't suggest that she does not really feel badly or that she is just trying to get your sympathy. Don't tell her to "just pray about it and read the Word more." Often a depressed person chooses portions of the Scriptures that reinforce feelings of loss and unworthiness. Any Scriptures given must be selected with care. (See Scriptures suggested later in this chapter.)

Empathize rather than sympathize with your wife. Sympathy can only reinforce her feelings of hopelessness. It may make her feel more helpless and may lower her already low self-esteem. Statements such as "It's so awful that you are depressed," "You must feel miserable," and "How could this ever happen?" rarely help.

If your wife is having difficulty sleeping, suggest a warm bath before going to bed. Play some favorite music, or read an interesting book to her. Your involvement shows that you care.

If your wife loses interest in activities she normally enjoys, gently remind her of the past enjoyment she derived from the activities. Then firmly and positively insist that she become involved. Don't ask her if she would like to become involved; she might not know or care to respond. You could say, "I know you have not felt well in the past, but I feel you are entitled to some enjoyment. I think you might like this once we get started, and I would like to share this activity with you." Any activity such as window shopping, a social event, or calling a friend can be used. By getting involved, the person begins to break the destructive behavior patterns and this helps her gain energy and motivation.

If your wife begins to let her appearance go, don't just hint about the situation. Openly, clearly, and explicitly tell her that she will enjoy fixing herself up and perhaps will feel better for it.

Loss of confidence and self-esteem is common in depression. Never tease or lecture your wife about lack of confidence, and don't ignore it; it must be faced. Help her look for past accomplishments in her life. Get her to focus on what she was able to accomplish prior to the onset of the depression. At this point you are trying to overcome her hopelessness. Don't join in the self-pity but respond by saying, "Perhaps you can't do anything the way you did before, but let's talk about the things you still do well. What do you think they are?" If she says, "I can't do anything," gently name some things she can do, or draw them out of her. Be persistent and steady in your responses.

By following these principles, it is possible for us to fulfill the biblical teaching of empathy and encouragement to one another. Galatians 6:2 says, "Bear (endure, carry) one another's burdens and troublesome moral faults, and in this way fulfill and observe perfectly the law of Christ, the Messiah, and complete what is lacking [in your obedience to it]." (*AMP*). Note also 1 Thessalonians 5:14: "And we earnestly beseech you, brethren, admonish (warn and seriously advise) those who are out of line—the loafers, the disorderly and the unruly; encourage the timid and fainthearted, help and give your support to the weak souls [and] be very patient with everybody—always keeping your temper" (*AMP*).

Some of the passages to share with a depressed person are Psalms 27:1-3; 37:1-7; Isaiah 26:3; 40:28-31; 43:1-3.

WHAT DO YOU THINK?

1. How do you respond when your spouse is angry, depressed, sad, or worried?

2. How do you respond when you feel angry, depressed, sad or worried?

3. Have you noticed a change in your emotional responses during the past six months? If so, in what way?

4. Which emotion would you like assistance with at the present time?

The following paraphrase of 1 Corinthians 13 will help a person "tune in" to God's love. Try reading it out loud every morning and evening. You may want to read it to your spouse.

Because God Loves Me
A Paraphrase of 1 Corinthians 13

Because God loves me He is slow to lose patience with me.

Because God loves me He takes the circumstances of my life and uses them in a constructive way for my growth.

Because God loves me He does not treat me as an object to be possessed and manipulated.

Because God loves me He has no need to impress me with how great and powerful He is because He is God nor does He belittle me as His child in order to show me how important He is.

Because God loves me He is for me. He wants to see me mature and develop in His love.

Because God loves me He does not send down His wrath on every little mistake I make—of which there are many.

Because God loves me He does not keep score of all my sins and then beat me over the head with them whenever He gets the chance.

Because God loves me He is deeply grieved when I do not walk in the ways that please Him because He sees this as evidence that I don't trust Him and love Him as I should.

Because God loves me He rejoices when I experience His power and strength and stand up under the pressures of life for His Name's sake.

Because God loves me He keeps on working patiently with me even when I feel like giving up and can't see why He doesn't give up with me, too.

Because God loves me He keeps on trusting me when at times I don't even trust myself.

Because God loves me He never says there is no hope for me; rather, He patiently works with me, loves me and disciplines me in such a way that it is hard for me to understand the depth of His concern for me.

Because God loves me He never forsakes me even though many of my friends might.

Because God loves me He stands with me when I have reached the rock bottom of despair, when I see the real me and compare that with His righteousness, holiness, beauty and love. It is at a moment like this that I can really believe that God loves me.

Yes, the greatest of all gifts is God's perfect love![4]

WHAT'S YOUR PLAN?

1. Which emotions have been difficult for you to handle in the past? How will a baby affect them? What will you do now prior to the baby's birth to strengthen this area of your life?

2. What can you do at this time to insure father's involvement with the baby during the first three months?

3. Develop a specific plan of action to follow if the four-day blues should occur.

Notes

All material quoted is used by permission.
1. Adapted from Lee Salk and Rita Kramer, *How to Raise a Human Being* (New York: Random House, Inc., 1969), pp. 83-85.
2. Adapted from Tracy Hotchner, *Pregnancy and Childbirth* (New York: Avon Books, 1979), pp. 520-530.
3. Michael Newton, M.D., "New Baby! Why So Sad?" *Family Health/Today's Health*, May, 1976, pp. 17,64; K.L.K. Trick, M.D., "Psychological Problems Following Birth and Miscarriage," *Nursing Mirror*, July 10, 1975, pp. 61,62; Joy Princeton Clausen and others, "Childrearing and the Nursing Process," in *Maternity Nursing Today* (New York: McGraw-Hill, 1973), pp. 588-591.
4. Dick Dickinson, Inter-Community Counseling Center, Long Beach, CA.

The Wonderful Creation

Behold, children are a gift of the Lord;
The fruit of the womb is a reward.
Like arrows in the hand of a warrior,
So are the children of one's youth.
How blessed is the man whose quiver is full of them;
They shall not be ashamed,
When they speak with their enemies in the gate.
—Psalm 127:3-5

Prenatal Development

From the moment of conception, a child develops remarkably fast. Within a few short hours the cells begin to form the baby inside its mother. They divide at a very rapid pace; so rapidly that by the end of the second week the embryo consists of approximately 150 cells, each beginning to serve a special function. By the twenty-first day of development, the heart of the embryo begins to beat within the mother. The brain and spinal cord have already formed. These vital developments do not take place after the child is a 7-pound, 20-inch human being, but when the fetus is about 25 millimeters long or about one tenth of an inch. By the end of the fourth week the entire embryo is formed and the legs and arms have begun to form.

It is no wonder that God has regarded children as one of His most wonderful creations. Edith Deen says this about the unborn child:

"From the time of his conception, a Hebrew child was rightly regarded as one of God's most wonderful creations. No one knew exactly how the tiny embryo grew. One writer declared, 'As thou knowest not . . . how the bones do grow in the womb of her that is with child, even so thou knowest not the works of God who maketh all' (Ecclesiastes 11:5).

"The marvelous development of the child in his mother's womb seemed to be an extraordinary manifestation of God's goodness, for which the Psalmist offered his praise: 'Thou hast covered me (knit me together) in my mother's womb. I will praise thee, for I am fearfully and wonderfully made' (Psalm 139:13-14)."[1]

During the second month of pregnancy the backbone has begun to form and approximately eight vertebrae are in place. The nervous system and spinal canal also are forming. The spinal canal is the channel through which the nervous system proceeds from the brain and into the entire body. The heart is still beating with intense regularity. The head is forming with a cavity for a mouth and the passage leading downward into the digestive tract. Impressions appear where eyes and ears will eventually be. The infant's sex is determined as early as the seventh week, when the embryo is only a quarter of an inch long. The muscles begin to respond to nerve impulses, causing the infant to begin movement; although the mother does not feel it move until between three and a half and four months.

By the end of the second month the fetus is a well-proportioned, small, full-scale baby at less than an inch long, with a face, eyes that are hidden behind closed lids, ears that function, a mouth that opens, lips, tongue, chest, abdomen, arms, legs, and hands partially formed. Its lungs are forming; bone cells have begun to develop. This half-inch embryo is making the transition to fetus weighing only one-thirtieth of an ounce. Job may not have understood the specifics of the growth process, but he understood the marvels which God had created in the development of the unborn child. Job says in 10:8-12: "Thy hands fashioned and made me altogether, and wouldst Thou destroy me? Remember now, that Thou hast made me as clay; and wouldst Thou turn me into dust again? Didst Thou not pour me out like milk, and curdle me like cheese; clothe me with skin and flesh, and knit me together with bones and sinews? Thou hast granted me life and lovingkindness, and Thy care has preserved my spirit.''

By the end of the third month circulation has begun inside the fetus. Its digestive tract is functioning, and amniotic fluid is swallowed and urinated back out. Its nervous system is also functioning completely with brain signals and muscle responses. Its joints have begun to move, and its tiny fingers begin to curl. It has grown to three inches in length and weighs approximately one ounce.

Even prenatally the infant is obviously a human being—it moves and functions. The heart is beating between 117 and 157 beats per minute—it is active. Edith Deen has this to say:

"How or when an unborn child became endowed with the central element of his being, with his soul, no one could say. Some of the transcendent mystery and grandeur is expressed in the old story of Adam's creation when God 'breathed into his nostrils the breath of life, and man became a living soul' (Genesis 2:7). The people of Israel firmly believed that the unborn child's body and soul were fused together by the Lord, who 'stretcheth forth the heavens, and layeth the foundation of the earth, and formeth the spirit of man within him' (Zechariah 12:1).

"Some of the prophets declared that the Lord had ordained them as early as their prenatal period. During this time He prepared them to be His spokesmen. Isaiah explained his call to be a prophet in these words: 'The Lord called me from the womb, from the body of my mother he named my name. He made my mouth like a sharp sword, in the shadow of his hand he hid me; he made me a polished arrow, in his quiver he hid me away' (Isaiah 49:1-2, *RSV*).''[2]

During the fourth month a mother may begin to feel the fetus moving. Its length is now approximately seven inches, and its weight has increased to about four ounces.

By the beginning of the fifth month the mother feels the movements of the infant within her. By the end of the sixth month the hair, eyebrows, and eyelashes have begun to form, and its eyelids can open. Nails have formed at the end of tiny fingers. The infant is coated with vernix to protect the fetus from the watery world in which it lives. By the end of the sixth month the fetus is now nearly a foot long, weighing about one and a half pounds.

During the seventh month the fetus may begin to practice thumb sucking. It has grown to approximately 15 inches and weighs approximately two-and-a-half pounds.

During the eighth month the infant grows rapidly to approximately sixteen and a half inches and weighs between four and four and a half pounds.

During the last month before delivery the infant gains another two to two and a half pounds. Through the placenta it receives antibodies that provide immunity to whatever diseases the mother has had and help protect the infant during the first few months of life.

Because of the rapid development a fetus experiences during its nine months in the womb, it is extremely important that the mother practice good nutrition. Tracy Hotchner reminds parents of the following:

"There is no way to stress enough the importance of nutrition. Eating well is essential to your comfort while you're pregnant, for a better labor and delivery, and for a healthy, intelligent baby. If you think about nothing else while you're pregnant, please think about what you're putting in your mouth and what effect it will have. . . .

"There are many benefits to good nutrition, starting with the fact that you will feel better and look better if you eat well. The foremost benefit is that good nutrition helps prevent stillbirth and low birth weight. . . . Another benefit is that there is a direct relationship between prenatal nutrition and a lack of complications during pregnancy, labor, and delivery. A good diet creates a strong uterus, which helps insure a good labor with efficient contractions. Good nutrition has also been shown to prevent infections and anemia in the mother. A well-balanced diet, rich in protein, has also been linked with a lower incidence of toxemia of late pregnancy. . . .

"There are two periods of rapid growth of the baby's brain cells: at 20 weeks gestation and at 36 weeks gestation (about one month before birth). The human brain develops most rapidly in the last part of the pregnancy and the cell division in the brain is impaired if there is malnutrition at that time. Inadequate food intake can cause an irreversible deficit in the number of brain cells but it can also mean malformed cells and impaired interconnections between cells. The latter results in learning problems and poor motor coordination.

"The message should be very clear: Do not go even 24 hours without food. Do not skip meals. People who don't know any better are compromising a baby's intelligence and physical coordination. That is a tragedy. But if you know the results of poor nutrition and you don't eat well, that is a crime."[3]

Physical Development of the New Baby

Don't be surprised or disappointed when the doctor hands you that beautiful newborn infant for the first time—especially if it is in the delivery room—if he or she does not seem to be all that he is cracked up to be. The baby may not seem as beautiful as you may have thought he should be, but give the baby a few hours and watch the difference in his appearance. You wouldn't look too good either if you had been sitting in a bathtub filled with warm water for nine months. Your skin would be wrinkled and white, and you might look like a little old lady who was just squeezed out of a tube of toothpaste. The infant lives in the amniotic sac for nine months in tepid water, and then suddenly it is pushed and squeezed out of the birth canal and into the world. It is not unusual for its head to appear elongated or lopsided as a result of pressure during birth.

A newborn infant may have a thick crop of hair or none at all. Either is normal. The baby with lots of hair could lose it, and the bald baby may gain a full head of hair. Don't worry, hair will come in. You may also note a newborn baby's head seems too large for his body. The infant's head is much larger than the rest of his body, but the body will catch up in a very short period of time. There will be two soft spots on the top of the skull called fontanels, one just above the brow and the other near the crown of the head. As the baby grows, both of these will close. The baby's eyes may be blue or gray, but this is not necessarily the final color. Don't be concerned if the eyes cross; the baby is still forming and his muscles are still not complete. The feet appear much more complete than they really are. At this point only one real bone has formed in the heel, and the rest is only cartilege. The average infant weighs 6 to 8 pounds at birth and averages 18 to 22 inches in length.

You will be amazed at how small a newborn is. To be able to hold the baby in one hand and to realize that this small bundle eventually will grow into an adult is beyond imagination; it is enough to bring tears to the most hearty man.

Your baby's legs might be slightly bowed or they might seem quite short in comparison with the rest of his body. The legs develop much more slowly, even during the prenatal portion of development. They are much farther away from the source of nutrition and blood supply, but they will catch up. The bowing is normal and has nothing to do with what the child will be like once he starts to walk.

The baby's skin is thin—you can even see its veins—and dry, and may be covered with soft hair. The newborn infant may be covered with vernix, white cheesy material that protects its skin while it is in the amniotic sac. The hospital staff will clean the baby off and your son or daughter will be magnificently beautiful with soft, white skin—or he may be red faced with pudgy cheeks. His nose may appear very flat, and he may have a very short neck.

The baby's hands are usually held in a tight fist, but you will notice how perfectly formed they are. Each joint works, and each finger has a tiny, paper-thin nail.

Each child develops at his own pace. Don't be upset if your child does not look just like the one next to yours in the nursery. God has created each person as a unique being; it is so even from the moment of birth. Your child has a lot of time to grow and develop and to change. Each day, each week, each month will bring about differences in looks and appearance that will amaze even you. Or, perhaps the changes will come so slowly that they are undetectable until you go back and compare early photos to see the differences.

Behavioral Development

The newborn baby's behavior doesn't follow any precise schedule or format. All the things that have been written about a newborn's life or schedule are averages, so one infant may wake every hour to be fed and the next may not wake up for four to five hours. Whatever the case, it does require some adjustment on the part of the new parents.

What are some of the characteristics parents should look for in the newborn infant? The newborn normally retains its fetal position—arms and legs curled up toward his chest—with his knees slightly bent and his legs slightly bowed. If you place an object in the infant's hands, he will grasp the object reflexively and not be aware of noises and stimuli coming from his environment. He will not pay attention to what is going on around him. He may sleep from 20 to 24 hours a day or may not want to sleep at all. The baby's muscles are oriented primarily to mass activity such as rolling, twisting, and squirming movements of the large muscles as opposed to any fine muscle control. The infant may be able to hold his head up a few seconds while lying on his stomach, if not immediately after birth most probably at the end of the first month. Babies see quite readily, much more than has ever previously been believed. Babies like human faces and will look at a face longer and harder than any other object placed before them. By the end of the first month the infant will show a definite sleep and wake pattern and the beginning of an eating pattern.

Don't be surprised if during the first month there is no schedule and if Mom or Dad is up constantly taking care of the new baby. It is very important during this time to be sure that both Mom and Dad are getting enough rest for themselves, trading off feeding shifts and perhaps having some outside help during the first month to aid with the care of the baby so that periods of rest are available. During that first month the baby's physical characteristics may allow him to hold his head off the bed for a few moments while lying on his stomach, and he may follow an object with his eyes for a short distance. Normally he will enjoy looking at faces and may even smile when you smile and play with him.

Dr. Alvin Eden emphasizes the importance of preparing to meet the changes a newborn brings to a home and family:

"There is no question that a new baby will make many revolutionary changes in your life-style. Life at home now becomes an entirely new experience. Your new baby should bring a lot of joy and happiness into your house. She need not cause you extra tension and worry. Unfortunately, however, a good many new parents are totally unprepared and uninformed about what to really expect from their newborn. This lack of preparation results in tired and harassed mothers and fathers, leaving very little time or energy to really enjoy a new baby.

"As a pediatrician with long experience, I know very well how important the first few months of a baby's life are in establishing a baby's behavior patterns and personality. Everybody agrees that infants flourish and thrive in relaxed and peaceful households as do their parents."[4]

What should you expect in the way of developmental characteristics during the first year with your newborn? In order to give a brief overview, the infant's characteristics are divided into four major groups:

1. Use of his or her entire body
2. Use of hands and eyes
3. Use of ears and voice
4. His or her behavior with other people.

The resource from which this material is taken is entitled *Infant Care*, U.S. Department of Health, Education and Welfare publication number OCD 73-15 available from the Government Printing Office.[5] This booklet is the number one best-seller in the entire U.S. Government Printing Office and has been for a number of years. Following are some of the characteristics that you may see in your child during his first year.

In its entire body development, an infant normally holds his head upright while lying on his stomach by three months of age. By four months of age he should be able to hold his head steady while you hold him in a sitting position. By five months he may be able to roll over from back to front or from front to back, and by eight months of age he will be able to sit without support when placed in a sitting position. By 11 months of age, he can get himself into a sitting position in the crib or on the floor. By eight months he will begin to support some of his own weight on his legs. By 10 months he should be able to stand while holding on. By 13 months he should be able to stand for a moment alone, and by 14 months he should be able to stand well alone. By 13 months your child may be holding on to furniture and walking and by 15 months of age be able to walk alone across the room.

An infant's use of hands and eyes includes the following characteristics. By six weeks of age he can follow an object for a short distance with his eyes. By four months he follows from one side of his head to the other with his eyes. By four months he can bring his hands together in front of him. By four and a half months he can grasp a rattle placed in his fingers and by seven and a half months pass a toy from one hand to another. By eight months he can grasp a small object like a raisin off of a flat surface, and by 10 months he can pick up small objects using his thumb and finger. By 12 months he can bring together two toys that he holds in his hands.

The infant's use of voice develops very quickly. You will find that your infant will pay attention to sounds around him by the time he is six weeks of age. He will also begin to make sounds other than just crying by this same age. By three and a half months of age your child will probably be laughing and beginning to learn how to squeal, and sometime between four and eight months when you speak to your child, he will begin to turn to your voice. By 10 months of age a child normally can say "Dada" or "Mama" or both, and by the time he is 14 months of age, "Dada" and "Mama" mean one specific person and not just any man or woman in general. He will begin to imitate the speech sounds you make by 11 months of age. If you have any irritating speech pattern that you don't want your child to repeat, now is the time to refrain from it. In our home an exaggerated "hi" was often heard. It was one of the first sounds our daughter was able to pick up on her own.

As the infant interacts with other people, you will find that a newborn infant loves to focus on a face. That is the most attractive image he can have, and it helps with parental infant bonding. Allow him to see your face rather than just hear your voice. You will find that a newborn infant will readily begin to recognize Mom and Dad by the time he is two months of age. By five months of age he will be smiling on his own, and by 10 months he will pull back a toy that is in his hands. By nine months he will be reaching for toys that are out of his reach. By eight months he will be feeding himself crackers. By 16 months he should be drinking from a cup. By the end of his first year, he will be able to play peek-a-boo, patty-cake, and play with a ball on the floor.

Don't force your child to learn. Learning at this point is primarily by imitation, and formal learning takes place later on in the child's development. Don't expect him to learn too much too soon.

WHAT DO YOU THINK?

1. List several areas in which a child develops while growing physically.

2. Of the characteristics of children at different ages we have described, which do you feel is most important? Which would your spouse say is most important?

3. You probably have listed emotional development as being one way in which your child will develop. List five ways that you can provide for your child's emotional development. Be specific.

    (1)
    (2)
    (3)
    (4)
    (5)

Children are products of two very powerful factors that influence their development. One is heredity and the other is the environment in which he or she lives. It is very easy to see what our children have inherited. We see the physical attributes with which God has endowed them. We see their daily growth. We see their height and weight, their build, their coloring. Each of these characteristics is easily noticed, but our environment and role as parents are equally as important in the development of our child. His emotions, temperament, personality, and spiritual life are determined to a large extent by these environmental factors.

Providing Emotional Needs

Each child needs to develop emotionally as well as physically. What provisions will you and your spouse make for that development? What emotional needs must be met by parents? From the moment your new baby arrives in its home, God asks that we meet his emotional needs. There are several that are discussed in this chapter: every child needs to be loved; he needs to feel secure—to feel that he is not helpless—but he does need to feel that protection is available to him; he needs to be nourished—not only physically but also emotionally; a child needs to know that life is a positive experience, not one built on punishment; a child needs freedom but he also needs discipline or boundaries within which to live.

Probably the most important emotional need any child has is the need for love and affection. This seems to be a very obvious statement as most parents practice this instinctively. But many parents have a great deal of difficulty showing how they feel toward their child. Titus 2:4 reminds us that a mother should love her children. Older women are told to "encourage the young women to love their husbands, to love their children" (*NASB*).

Some parents are afraid to actively seek out and demonstrate the capacity which God has given them to love their children. It is wrong on the parents' part to assume a child knows how they feel and that it isn't necessary to demonstrate their affection for the child. A child needs to be told and shown how much he is loved. If parents are not capable of communicating affection to their child, or if the child doesn't experience affection coming from his parents, it would be easy for that child to feel that he is unlovable. A child of God feeling unlovable? How incongruous in the light of what the Scriptures teach, but how often this takes place in today's society! Once a child feels unloved or unlovable, then the door to his emotional development may be closed.

WHAT DO YOU THINK?

1. List five ways in which you could demonstrate love and affection for your child.

(1)

(2)

(3)

(4)

(5)

2. Of the five ways you listed, how many could your spouse participate in with you? Share your list with your spouse.

3. Are there any ways of demonstrating affection on your spouse's list that you would feel uncomfortable in doing with your own child?

One of the most important ways of demonstrating love and affection to a child is by natural and spontaneous physical contact—hugging, touching, embracing, or just holding. Howard Bessell says that being affectionate or touching "affectionately delivers four vital messages to your child simultaneously: 'I notice you, include you, endorse you and most of all, love you.' " In this way your loving embrace gives your child's self-image a powerful boost.

The interest that you take in your child also communicates love and affection to that child. Proverbs 5:1, "My son, give attention to my wisdom, incline your ear to my understanding," tells us that we understand our child and know what is best for him. But can we really understand or know what is best for our child if we do not know him or take an interest in him? Children love to talk with their parents. Are you a ready listener? Parents do not always have to respond to what their children are trying to communicate. The fact that you are interested and willing to listen will make him feel better about the day and especially about himself.

A second emotional need that children have is that of protection. Just as the shepherd guards his sheep, so also are parents to guard their children from physical dangers and emotional perils and from spiritual attack. In their role as protector, parents are to provide for their children: "Here for this third time I am ready to come to you, and I will not be a burden to you; for I do not seek what is yours, but you; for children are not responsible to save up for their parents, but parents for their children" (2 Cor. 12:14).

And Ephesians 6:4 says we are to nurture our children: "And, fathers, do not provoke your children to anger; but bring them up in the discipline and instruction of the Lord." Proverbs 22:6 reminds us that we are to train our children: "Train up a child in the way he should go, even when he is old he will not depart from it." Each of these will help our children feel that we are providing protection.

The parents' role in providing protection for their child is of emotional support so the child can meet head on the challenges and insecurity that life holds for him. This protection does not mean protecting our child from the possibilities of failure. Our child needs to understand that failure is all right; he is still accepted even though he is capable of making mistakes.

A third emotional need that children have is for a balance of freedom and restraint. Children need to be able to experience the world around them, but they also need to be limited or kept from doing harm to themselves or others. The Scriptures are clear that discipline is an important aspect of being a parent. Proverbs 19:18 tells us that parents should "discipline your son while there is hope, and do not desire his death."

A fourth emotional need of children is nourishment. Every child needs to feel wanted. Knowing that you want him gives him a basic security. Just as the shepherd loves and cares for his sheep and strives to meet their every need, so also—and more importantly—are parents to do the same. Ephesians 6:4 reminds us that one of our roles is nurturing a child. The best form of nourishment that we can provide our children is to let them know that we care and that they are important to us and that they are wanted. If their children are not wanted or desired, parents will never be able to hide this from them.

Our children need a positive experience from life itself. There is nothing sadder than counseling an adolescent who sees no reason for living, who experiences nothing positive out of life. His parents have not encouraged or loved him or shown emotion or met his emotional needs. Teenage suicide is very high in our society today, and much of the reason for this increase is that adolescents do not have a positive base from which to view life.

Another emotional need we all have is for a sense of humor in our home. When your child spills his milk for the fifteenth time can you laugh the way you did the first time? When a child discovers how to pull the cap off his milk bottle or grabs the cat's tail for the first time, hopefully we can laugh at these experiences.

Social development among infants begins with a very egocentric self. The child is interested only in having his own needs met—from birth through the first year. This is one reason why parents end up being so harried—they wonder if this child is ever going to give consideration to their needs. Between the ages of one and five children begin to progress slowly from the egocentric individual toward someone who can interact with other individuals. This progress begins by children playing alongside of others and eventually moving to the ability to play with other children.

A child's spiritual development is discussed in another chapter.

WHAT'S YOUR PLAN?

1. What is the greatest fear you have concerning your child's physical development?

You and your spouse should take time to discuss each other's fears. Arrange a time now when you can each share your fears and what you might do to overcome them.

2. When you finish this discussion, each of you should take your spouse's fear to the Lord. Then pray for the child that God will give you in your future. Begin to anticipate the gift that God may be preparing for your home.

Notes

All material quoted is used by permission.
1. Edith Deen, *Family Living in the Bible* (Old Tappan, NJ: Spire Books, 1969), p. 9.
2. *Ibid.*, p. 10.
3. Tracy Hotchner, *Pregnancy and Childbirth* (New York: Avon Books, 1979).
4. Alvin N. Eden, M.D., *Handbook for New Parents* (New York: Berkeley Publishing Corporation, 1978).
5. U.S. Department of Health, Education, and Welfare, *Infant Care*, publication number OCD 73-15 (Washington D.C.: Government Printing Office).

To Know the Love of Christ

The goal of family living—to know the love of Christ—is reflected in one of Paul's great prayers to the Ephesian church:

"For this reason, I bow my knees before the Father, from whom every family in heaven and on earth derives its name, that He would grant you, according to the riches of His glory, to be strengthened with power through His Spirit in the inner man; so that Christ may dwell in your hearts through faith; and that you, being rooted and grounded in love, may be able to comprehend with all the saints what is the breadth and length and height and depth, and to know the love of Christ which surpasses knowledge, that you may be filled up to all the fulness of God. Now to Him who is able to do exceeding abundantly beyond all that we ask or think, according to the power that works within us, to Him be the glory in the church and in Christ Jesus to all generations forever and ever. Amen" (Eph. 3:14-21).

WHAT DO YOU THINK?

1. What are five things that you could do to communicate the love of Christ to your child when he is one month old?

(1)

(2)

(3)

(4)

(5)

2. What are five things that you and your spouse could do that would contribute to the spiritual development of your child when he is six months old?

(1)

(2)

(3)

(4)

(5)

3. List two additional things that you and your spouse could do to encourage the spiritual development of your child when he is one year old.

(1)

(2)

Parents are a model to children of what our heavenly Parent is like. Bruce Narramore, in his book *Parenting with Love and Limits,* says this about what the modeling parents do for their children:

"In establishing the family God has provided a visible model of the way in which He relates to us. In other words, God designed the family to teach us in a tangible, first-hand way about Himself. Just as God uses the intimate relationship of husband and wife to illustrate Christ's relationship to the church (Eph. 5:22-33), children and parents represent our relationship to Him as our heavenly parent (Heb. 12:5-11). Although frequently overlooked, this is one of the most important purposes of the family. Children need experience with flesh-and-blood parents to help them grasp the spiritual truth that God is our heavenly Father.

"Richard Strauss put it this way:

" 'The point is well established in the Bible. God's parenthood and our parenthood are a great deal alike—at least they should be. . . . A person's image of God is often patterned after his image of his own parents, especially his father. If his parents were happy, loving, accepting, and forgiving, he finds it easier to experience a positive and satisfying relationship with God. But if his parents were cold and indifferent, he may feel that God is far away and disinterested in him personally. If his parents were angry, hostile, and rejecting he often feels that God can never accept him. If his parents were hard to please, he usually has the nagging notion that God is not very happy with him either.'

"Orphans and children of parents with seriously defective personalities often find it extremely difficult to develop a true concept of God. And if such children do gain an intellectual understanding of the character of God, they frequently have difficulty experiencing the fact that God loves them because their experience with earthly parents was so far removed from the biblical revelation concerning parent-child relations. Even children from 'normal' or 'healthy' homes are likely to have some false concepts of who God is, since we all fall short of God's character in some degree.

"One of the highest callings of Christian parents, then, is to build loving, sensitive, and honest relationships with their children so that later in life these children can freely turn to God the Father and readily accept His loving forgiveness.

"What an incentive this is for parents to grow! Although our problems and sins may interfere with our child's relationship with God, our consistent love lays a foundation for meaningful faith in God."[1]

John White, in *Parents in Pain*, says this about the parent in God's image:

"Let me restate the basic rule of parenting: As God is to me so must I be to my children. As he has dealt with me, so must I deal with them. Such kindness as he has shown me, such patience and forbearing, such intolerance of sin—these must I in turn show to those for whom I stand in place of God. For in my children's minds a concept of God is growing which is derived from my spouse and me, two powerful beings who gave them birth and who seem to rule over the cosmos of the home. Each time my children see a godlike attitude or action in their father or mother, the Holy Spirit will tell them, 'Now you can understand a little better what your Father in heaven is like.'

"Yet our striving to this higher goal must not be merely for our children's sake. Just as we are called to be holy because God is holy, so we are called to be parents because he is a parent, and that is reason enough. We were created in his image and to that image, even the image of God the Parent, we are called to be faithful."[2]

Husband-Wife Relationships

If parents are to be a model to their children of what God's relationship is to His church then what are you and your spouse going to model to your child? The Word of God uses a picture of the relationship between the bride and the bridegroom to model Christ's relationship to the church. The principles in that word picture indicate what parents can model to their children. It is very difficult to teach or train a newborn infant, but one way an infant learns is by imitating what he sees other people around him do. Therefore, your child may very well imitate your relationship to your spouse in his relationships with other people. Is this relationship one that you would be happy to have your child imitate?

WHAT DO YOU THINK?

1. How would you describe your marital relationship?

2. What are 10 positive characteristics of your relationship with your spouse?

(1)

(2)

(3)

(4)

(5)

(6)

(7)

(8)

(9)

(10)

3. What are three negative characteristics of your relationship with your spouse?

(1)

(2)

(3)

4. Looking at your list of positive characteristics, choose one that you would like to build into your child's life. If this characteristic were to become a part of your child's development, what benefits would your child derive?

5. Looking at your list of negative characteristics, choose one that you definitely do not want to see in your child's life. If it were a part of your child's character, what potential problems could he face in later life?

The relationship between husband and wife or mother and father is the closest relationship a child will observe. Therefore, it is very important that what the mother and father do in their relationship with each other is a positive influence on the child. Ephesians 5:22-32 describes the relationship between the bride and the bridegroom. There are several basic principles that come out of that description which can be applied to the relationship of fathers and mothers to their children.

Probably the most obvious principle in the relationship of the bride to the bridegroom is love—intense, wholehearted, unashamed love. That love relationship is best described in Scripture in 1 Corinthians 13. Let's take a look at that chapter and see whether you are demonstrating the characteristics of love to your spouse. These verses indicate that love consists of many elements, negative and positive.

WHAT DO YOU THINK?

Tell one way in which you have demonstrated love toward your spouse during the past week in each of the following areas:

1. Love suffers long—endures offenses, is not hasty, waits for the Lord to right all wrong.

2. Love is kind—not inconsiderate, seeks to help, is constructive, blesses when cursed, helps when hurt, demonstrates tenderness.

3. Love is not envious but content—is not jealous of another person's success or competition.

4. Love is not arrogant, but humble—is not haughty but lowly and gracious.

5. Love is not boastful, but reserved—does not show off, try to impress, or want to be the center of attraction.

6. Love is not rude, but courteous.

7. Love is not selfish, but self-forgetful.

8. Love is not irritable, but good-tempered.

9. Love is not vindictive or wrathful, but generous.

10. Love does not delight in bringing another person's sins to light, but rejoices when another person obeys the truth.

11. Love is not rebellious, but brave; conceals rather than exposes another person's wrongdoing to others.

12. Love is not suspicious but trustful, not cynical, makes every allowance, looks for an explanation that will show the best in others.

13. Love is not despondent, but hopeful; does not give up because it has been deceived or denied.

14. Love is not conquerable, but invincible—can outlast problems.

In the husband-wife relationship God has called the bride and bridegroom to the highest of interpersonal relationships. The involvement between the husband and wife brings them to the point of being one flesh, and out of that one flesh our offspring arrives. Out of that highest of personal relationships a new relationship is developed through the birth of our children. Just as the bridegroom is responsible for protecting his bride as Christ protected His church, so are the parents responsible for protecting their child from the sin and pitfalls of life by teaching the child the ways of the Lord. If a child is brought up in a home that is filled with sin and impurity, that model may be what the child chooses as a life-style in later life, but if we as parents protect the purity of our children, not only in their relationships with other people, but also in their relationships with the Lord, then that child has an opportunity to choose a model of spiritual development that is positive and constructive. The young child's spiritual development is built on natural trust, absolute faith, and a readiness to believe.

Because of this natural trust, a parent can encourage or discourage spiritual development of a child at an early age. The kind of parents you will be may be reflected in the kind of husband or wife you are.

Negative Modeling

Let's take a look at the kind of relationships husbands and wives my be modeling before their children. These relationships may be depicting to your children a model of how they will perceive what God is like.

The first model is the perfectionistic parent, or his opposite, the parent who could not care less. A perfectionistic husband, wife, or parent is never satisfied. He feels that even the best could have been a little better. Some wives, husbands, or children get the feeling that what they do or what their loved ones do, is never quite good enough. They should have won by a wider margin. When a person never accepts his own performance or the performances of his spouse or children he encourages guilt in himself and in them, and a sense of failure.

On the other hand, a parent who could not care less is *always* satisfied and therefore displays disinterest. The parent's overriding ambition is his own comfort. Any time he spends with his children usually involves his own interest and is at his own convenience. He doesn't like or dislike his children; he just does not care about them.

God is not like either of these examples. He cares a great deal for each of us. And although He is involved in our lives constantly He does not expect performance greater than we are able to give. The Lord controls His children, and He encourages parents to control their children "with all dignity" (1 Tim. 3:4).

A second model is one of rejection as opposed to acceptance. A rejecting parent may not even want his loved ones around him. He makes excuses to be away from the children and maybe even from his spouse. He puts them off, and gives them the feeling that they are not even worthy of him. He often demands respect.

An accepting person, on the other hand, wants to be with his family and chooses to be with them in their world as well as in his. He can initiate love and affection, and can also accept it. Can your spouse talk to you without fear of being ostracized or rejected?

We live in an imperfect world and all of us are imperfect. Standards are important but must be realistic and obtainable. Even the most consistent person will have an off day. The home atmosphere is the place where failure and lapses can be turned into learning experiences through acceptance and encouragement.

A third model is the overprotective as opposed to the underprotective parent. Overprotective parents do not trust their children. Perhaps they are not sure they have done a good job in rearing them. Although the parent means well and loves his children very much, he does not distinguish between doing things *with* them and doing things *for* them.

Many husband-wife relationships are damaged because an overly-protective spouse keeps the other person from finding some degree of independence. Some parents, like some spouses, do not want to "let go and let grow."

The underprotective individual is just the opposite. He believes so strongly in the school of hard knocks that he fails to support and encourage his family when support is appropriate. He is unsympathetic and seems hard and uncaring. He is like the father who named his boy Sue so the boy would have to learn to defend himself. God is neither overprotective nor underprotective. He teaches the way in which His children should go. He allows them the freedom to make responsible choices.

Some marriages are characterized by an overindulgent spouse who believes that love must be bought or earned. This type person is willing to give his spouse everything but himself. Frequently, we may become overindulgent toward our spouse because we feel insecure or have a feeling of losing him or her.

The opposite husband-wife relationship is one in which one of the spouses is stingy and puts his own interest ahead of others. His possessions have become symbols of work. He has had such a hard time obtaining his present status that thrift has become a rigid habit. He may be reluctant to share not only his financial resources, but also his love, interests, fear, concern, and time.

In what ways is your spouse overindulgent? Are there specific situations where he or she purchases your affection? What might your spouse be withholding from you? What is he not willing to share? God's relationship to His children is that He provides for His children. He is neither stingy nor overindulgent but desires to meet the realistic needs of each child (See 2 Cor. 12:14).

The last model is the overpermissive, and its opposite, the legalistic person. The overpermissive parent or spouse is afraid of stifling the child's creativity or personality or future. Many overpermissive individuals are simply afraid of asserting themselves. They may not like what their children or spouse is doing, but they have not learned how to say no, how to communicate their feelings, and how to "care enough to confront."

The legalistic individual, though, at the opposite of the scale, is also a person who feels insecure in making decisions. He allows a code, a set of rules, or other outside authority to determine his decisions. This kind of person gets anxious when there is no precedent governing the situation. He is very intolerant of others' differences. This intolerance usually comes through in both verbal and nonverbal behavior. God nurtures His children rather than coercing or applying a legalistic code. He trains His children (see Prov. 22:6) and disciplines His children (see Prov. 19:18), and understands His children and what is best for them (Prov. 5:1). And He wants His children to follow His example in their own families.

To encourage the spiritual development of your child, it is important that you provide consistency in all aspects of his life. We need to let our children know that we are trustworthy individuals, that we are available to meet their needs. We must be consistent in providing security for our children. Some parents are inconsistent. They live by the do-as-I-say-and-not-as-I-do model. Since we as parents are models of what God is, what would your children think if they were to see you cheat on your income tax, fish without a license, or make promises which you have no intention of keeping? Is this the model that God has called you to—to teach your children it is okay to cheat, steal, or lie as long as they are not caught?

Positive Modeling

The godly models are parents who realize that the only way their children will understand God is through their relationships with their parents. They are not playing God for their children but are representing God to that child as best they can. God's attributes therefore become important to them. Being conformed to the image of Jesus is a way of loving their children as well as a way of following Christ.

WHAT DO YOU THINK?

1. What type of model will you present to your children?

2. Is Jesus Christ reflected in how you treat your spouse? In how your spouse treats you?

3. List 10 ways in which your spouse reflects or conforms to the image of Jesus Christ on a daily basis.
   (1)
   (2)

(3)
(4)
(5)
(6)
(7)
(8)
(9)
(10)

4. What are two areas that you would like to work on in your life that would help you to conform to the image of Christ and thereby give your child a better model of what his or her spirituality can become?

(1)
(2)

The following list will help you to provide an atmosphere in your home conducive to encouraging spiritual development in your children. Parents are the mirror to a child to let him know what he is really like. Parents who are proud of, have confidence in, and like their children are strengthening their spiritual development and helping them to develop inner peace. One of our most important tasks is helping children to learn to appreciate themselves as worthwhile human beings.

As parents we can:

• Love and accept a child as he is from the day he is born.

• Respect individual differences and appreciate each child's unique capacities.

• Show affection—*physically* by cuddling a baby or young child, and by hugging an older child, or even just patting him on the back; *verbally* through our choice of words and our tone of voice.

• Really listen when a child talks to us. Listening attentively gives insight into how he feels, builds rapport, and gives a child a sense of significance.

• Help a child see himself accurately so he can appreciate his strengths and accept his limitations.

• Set realistic expectations so a child can feel adequate to meet them. Inferiority results from out-of-reach goals set by perfectionistic parents and other adults.

- Provide for productive and creative work so he can do something he can be proud of. (Don't do it for him.)
- Help a child have successes—to do things in which he can succeed. Stress the wisdom of doing the best he can rather than trying to be a perfectionist.
- Praise more than criticize. Appreciate good points more often than nagging at faults, but be wary of overpraise. A child also needs to know he is not perfect.
- Set limits so a child knows for sure what gets our approval and disapproval. The worst feeling for a child is lack of control or disinterest of parents.
- Provide acceptable outlets for releasing tensions and angry feelings.
- Treat a child with respect and consideration. Children learn what they live.
- Enjoy each child and let him know we enjoy him. This makes him feel worthy.

WHAT'S YOUR PLAN?

1. From the list above, choose two areas that you would like to model to your spouse in the week ahead.

   (1)
   (2)

2. List three things that you can do to model the characteristic that would help to build your spouse's spiritual development.

   (1)
   (2)
   (3)

To conclude our thoughts on spiritual development, John White has this to share with parents:

"Was I willing, like God, to give the gift of life whatever the consequences might be, no matter how my child might choose to use that life? A hundred ugly possibilities flashed on the screen of my mind. A growing fear filled me. I was asking God to let me bring life into being. He was telling me I would not have control of what the fruit of my body might do with the life I gave. Was I still willing to give life to someone who might bring me humiliation, pain, disgrace?

"The question is basic to an understanding of all human relationships, not only to those of parent and child. We may teach; we may admonish; we may train; we may discipline; we may love. But unless in the case of a child we see him or her as much more than an extension of ourselves, we have not begun to learn what life is all about.

"In a moment of terrible despair and grief have you ever wished that one of your children had never been born? Or have you wished that he or she might conveniently die or disappear? How many times have you cried, 'I just cannot take any more'? Perhaps your pain and shame may have been made worse by the fact that you had yet to learn the most basic rule of all. You cannot ever control another human being, even if that human being is your own child. You do not have the right to. You may discipline and teach; you may train; you may point the right course; you may 'shape behavior patterns'; you may reason; you may plead. But you cannot and may not ever control. God has placed your child's ultimate destiny within your child's own hands.

"It was not easy for me to say, 'Yes. Give me the power to beget another child . . . whatever course that child may eventually choose in life.' But I said it. And I meant it. When I got to my feet I was not the same person as when I knelt down.

"The insight I was given on that sunny afternoon in Paris has not shielded me from parental suffering. But it has given me a basic guideline, a rope to hold on to in the dark, a way to grope forward when I could not see ahead. It was my first (but by no means my last) lesson in what being a parent means."[3]

Notes

All material quoted is used by permission.
1. Bruce Narramore, *Parenting with Love and Limits* (Grand Rapids: Zondervan Publishing House, 1979), pp. 28-30; Richard Strauss, *Confident Children and How They Grow* (Wheaton, IL: Tyndale House Publishers, 1975), pp. 23,24 as quoted in Narramore, p. 29.
2. John White, *Parents in Pain* (Downers Grove, Illinois: Inter-Varsity Press, 1979), pp. 209,210.
3. *Ibid.*, pp. 57,58.

What If...?

When I returned from a five-day camp with our church senior high group I was anxious to see my wife. I called the house from my office at the church. My mother-in-law answered the phone and said, "Joyce is all right, Norm. She's at the hospital. She had a miscarriage yesterday." I quickly called the hospital and talked with Joyce. She was all right. I sat in my chair for a while a bit stunned and sad. We hear about miscarriages all the time—happening to other people. But it feels so much different when it happens to you. With or without warning, it is still a loss.

Three years later we sat in a doctor's office at the UCLA Medical Clinic waiting for the neurologist's diagnosis for our son Matthew. Matthew was a year and a half old but was very slow and was having grand mal seizures. The diagnosis came—brain damage and improper brain formation, which has come to mean profound mental retardation.

Some children are born handicapped; some become handicapped. Some children die. We hear about it all the time happening to other people, but it feels so much different when it happens to us.

Prepare for the Unexpected

As you prepare for parenthood, prepare for the unexpected. There will be unexpected and often life-changing events. God's

Word is the stabilizing element that will help you through the unexpected. Consider Romans 5:3: "Moreover—let us also be full of joy now! Let us exult and triumph in our troubles and rejoice in our suffering knowing that pressure and affliction and hardship produce patient and unswerving endurance" (*AMP*).

The word *exult* means "leap for joy" or "leap up." This passage in Romans 5 is actually a description of the results of justification. We who are Christians can respond in this manner because of our relationship with God through Jesus Christ.

A second passage that is a base for parenthood is James 1:2,3 "Consider it wholly joyful, my brethren, whenever you are enveloped in or encounter trials of any sort, or fall into various temptations. Be assured and understand that the trial and proving of your faith bring out endurance and steadfastness and patience" (*AMP*).

The word *consider* means "an internal attitude of the heart or mind that causes the trial and the circumstance of life to affect us adversely or beneficially." The verb tense here means a decisiveness of action, not a simple resignation or giving up to "that's the way it is." Each of us has a choice of how to respond to the difficulties we will encounter. Remember the Old Testament character Job. He suffered and cried out, "Why?" If we have a miscarriage or a handicapped child, we will probably ask the same question.

Parents will find their life-style totally changed because of the presence of a handicapped child. Their faith may grow through the experience or it may diminish. Many parents, after years have gone by, have been able to identify positive results of the handicapped child's presence. But wholeness for any child is a natural desire.

What If Your Child Is Handicapped?

No parent expects his child to be handicapped, permanently maimed, disabled, or sick for a prolonged period. But it happens; and regardless of the specific problems, parents experience the same responses—anger, denial, shock, disbelief, and depression. Even a miscarriage can bring these same responses.

When a child has a physical or mental disability, parents react typically by searching from doctor to doctor for a new diagnosis.

Some parents spend so much time looking for a solution to their child's problem that they neglect their own needs. Some parents believe their child's problem is a punishment from God for their own sin or lack of faith. Parents begin to take responsiblity for the handicap or illness. They may feel the tragedy is a reflection on their own worth. They may ask, "Was there a hereditary defect? On whose side of the family was it? Who had the defective genes?" "Perhaps we had the wrong doctor," some say or, "Perhaps we didn't follow his advice." Blaming someone is a common reaction.

There can even be feelings of resentment and jealousy when parents compare their handicapped child with the normal children of others. Some handicaps can be overcome and corrected. Others cannot, and thus parents learn to accept the company of persistent sorrow. "Hope deferred makes the heart sick" (Prov. 13:12) is true in the lives of many parents.

When a child is born with or develops a handicap, it is natural for the parents to be overwhelmed. We tend to fear the worst rather than to hope. Often this reaction is a protective device; for if we hope and are disappointed, our hurt is so much deeper. No parent is ever fully prepared to be the parent of a handicapped child, and the surprise is painful.

When there is a problem, shock usually is the first response. Numbness and a lack of feeling set in. Then the various questions arise. "Why me?" "What will others think?" "How will we handle this?"

The second stage of normal reactions include denial and isolation. Mentally and emotionally we try to block out the reality of the situation and we search for alternate answers. We run from doctor to doctor to find someone who will say "nothing is wrong." Parents begin to see signs of progress whether there are any or not. This reaction creates false hope. This second stage is normal and allows parents to regroup and reconstruct their inner resources.

Anger and blame soon arrive upon the scene with explosive force. Anger must have an object so the parents begin to blame God, themselves, or each other. It is important for anger to be expressed and dealt with properly. Repressed anger can be harmful.

The fourth stage is bargaining. The parents try to make a deal—pleading with just about everyone. "If you heal my child, I will . . . " they say to God. "Doctor, are you sure? Couldn't you be wrong?" We even plead with the child: "Please do everything we ask you to do and you'll be well in no time." It is not uncommon for bargaining to reoccur from time to time as it is one way of retaining hope.

Depression is the next stage as the parents sense their helplessness. Apathy is common along with a feeling of "nothing matters, so why try; it's hopeless." Parents may experience difficulty in caring for the child at this time.

The final stage in this process is mourning and then acceptance. This sense of experiencing the loss leads to a gradual sense of acceptance of the situation of God's sovereignty.

If a couple has a handicapped child, the rest of the family is affected too. The father may feel all alone because the mother and child spend most of their time together. He may have to take on a second job or work overtime. The father may be ashamed of his child or of his own feelings. He may fear that the child may never be accepted at his old alma mater, especially if the father is very success oriented or athletic. Some fathers withdraw or even leave home because they cannot accept their severely handicapped child or because they cannot cope with having "fathered an imperfect child."

The mother often neglects other children and her husband. This neglect causes guilt and inconsistent emotions. Her physical and emotional stress is great and affects her ability to play her part in the normal marital relationship. She may even get very sick. Suicidal tendencies are not uncommon. In the beginning many mothers, especially those with a severely handicapped child, do not experience the joy of picking up their child and snuggling. They experience a great deal of anxiety when the child is sick, especially if he cannot communicate. The mother may insist that the child sleep in bed with her, thus "destroying the marriage bed." And once the child starts going to school, she may go to work to help out financially.

All of these difficulties place immeasurable stress on the marriage. Spouses usually go through the different stages of acceptance at different times, and one may accuse the other of being unfeeling. Desertion, separation, and divorce rates are extremely high among couples with a handicapped child. The strength of any marriage is always tested by a crisis. The health of the marriage and family greatly depends on both parents' acceptance of their "special child."[1]

What If She Has a Miscarriage?

A miscarriage can be a traumatic experience for some, yet it is a fairly common occurrence. Some studies indicate that one miscarriage occurs for every 10 pregnancies. Other studies show it happens once for every six pregnancies. An early miscarriage can feel no different physically than a heavy period.

The fear of the unknown can have an effect on the woman. Questions of, "What went wrong?" and "Did I do something wrong?" are common responses from a woman. Another reaction is the thought that something might be wrong with her or her mate.

A miscarriage is an emotional crisis. The feelings it arouses vary but include anger, guilt, fear, grief, helplessness, isolation, inadequacy, etc. This is a time for the couple to spend time with each other sharing feelings and giving comfort. The pattern found in Romans 12:15 is needed. "[Share others' joy], rejoicing with those who rejoice; and [share others' grief], weeping with those who weep" (*AMP*).

Be aware that others will make thoughtless comments.. "Oh, you can try again and have another," or, "There was something wrong with it" are common statements. Many people don't really know how to comfort another person and making inept comments is their way of trying to help. You may feel angry and isolated because of these remarks. This is a time to derive comfort from each other.

WHAT DO YOU THINK?

1. Describe a time in your life when you "exulted." Who did you share this with?

2. Have you experienced the various reactions to a problem as described in this chapter? If so, describe what you learned through this.

3. What do you think are the typical causes of a miscarriage?

4. What would your reaction and your spouse's reaction be to a miscarriage?

5. If you (or your spouse) were to experience a miscarriage, what could a person say to you that would be helpful?

Accepting the "What-Ifs"

As Christians we believe that God is sovereign, but when a pregnancy is terminated prematurely or a child is born with a handicap, we wonder why God's sovereignty did not extend to the child. We must remember that God is sovereign in everything. "O the depth of the riches and wisdom and knowledge of God! How unfathomable (inscrutable, unsearchable) are His judgments—His decisions! And how untraceable (mysterious, undiscoverable) are His ways—His methods, His paths!" (Rom. 11:33, *AMP*).

God *is* sovereign, even over the womb. He makes us and forms us. "Your hands have formed me and made me, would You turn around and destroy me? Remember [earnestly], I beseech You, that You have fashioned me as clay [out of the same earth-material, exquisitely and elaborately], and will You bring me into dust again? Have you not poured me out as milk and curdled me like cheese? You have clothed me with skin and flesh, and have knit me together with bones and sinews. You have granted me life and favor, and Your providence has preserved my spirit" (Job 10:8-12, *AMP*).

"For You did form my inward parts, You did knit me together in my mother's womb. My frame was not hidden from You, when I was being formed in secret and intricately and curiously wrought (as if embroidered with various colors) in the depths of the earth [a region of darkness and mystery]. Your eyes saw my unformed substance, and in Your book all the days of my life were written, before ever they took shape, when as yet there was none of them'' (Ps. 139:13,15,16, *AMP*).

"As you know not what is the way of the wind or how the spirit comes to the bones of the womb of a pregnant woman, even so you know not the work of God Who does all'' (Eccl. 11:5, *AMP*).

We have difficulty understanding what and why God does what He does. And we probably won't understand why. It is all right to complain. The heartache that is present calls for release. Parents do not have to like what has happened to their child and their feelings must be expressed in order to accept the child. God understands our hurt, anguish, and disappointment. He accepts our questioning, anger,and struggles. And remember, the problem did *not* occur because of sin in our life. "[Jesus'] disciples asked Him, Rabbi, who sinned, this man or his parents, that he should be born blind? Jesus answered, It was not that this man or his parents sinned; but he was born blind in order that the workings of God should be manifested—displayed and illustrated—in him'' (John 9:2,3, *AMP*).

Charles Swindoll describes an experience in his life in which God used several "special" children to display His works:

"While my family and I were up at Mount Hermon Family Camp in the Santa Cruz area last year that very thing happened. An amazing family was among us. Only one of the four children was 'normal.' Two were dwarfs and a third was born with only one heart valve. The two dwarfs walked with crutches and had to wear braces on their legs. The flesh of the boy with the congenital heart problem was not the normal color, due to poor circulation. No physician understands how he has lived to the age of twelve.

"All week long we talked and laughed and played together. They were a delightful family . . . no bitterness, no self-pity, not even the slightest glimmer of irritation. The last day of camp that family walked down in front around the fire and sang together, 'We're Something Special.' There wasn't a dry eye in the place. God used those three handicapped children and their supportive sister and parents to 'display His works' among us. As they sang I got a whole new appreciation for the way God allows families with handicapped children to model His truths.''[2]

WHAT DO YOU THINK?

1. Suppose a friend of yours has just received news that his child is handicapped. Write three helpful comments you could make to him.

(1)

(2)

(3)

2. What would some of your honest feelings be about spending time helping a friend with a physically deformed child?

3. What type of handicapped child would be most difficult for you to work with?

You may have children who are healthy but perhaps another couple, your friends, have a handicapped child. As members of the Body of Christ we are to reach out and minister to one another. Often we don't because we don't know what to say or do. Thus a couple already feeling isolated may feel even more isolated. As you go to minister to another couple, consider what Charles Swindoll says:

"Be real. As you reach out, admit your honest feelings to your friends. If the news stunned you, say so. If you suddenly feel tears coming, cry. If you are overwhelmed with pity and compassion, admit it. You may be a Christian with a firm hope in a life hereafter,

but you're also human. Don't hide that. It may be through that gate a path of friendship will develop.

"Be quiet. Your presence, not your words, will be most appreciated. The thick mantle of grief has fallen upon your friend, bringing dark, unexplainable sorrow. An abundance of words and attempts to instruct will only reveal an insensitive spirit to the grieving. The Joe Baylys, in the course of several years, lost three of their children. In his book, *The View from a Hearse,* he shares his honest feelings when one of the children died:

" 'I was sitting, torn by grief, someone came and talked to me of God's dealings, of why it happened, of hope beyond the grave. He talked constantly. He said things I knew were true.

" 'I was unmoved, except to wish he'd go away. He finally did.

" 'Another came and sat beside me. He didn't talk. He didn't ask me leading questions. He just sat beside me for an hour and more, listened when I said something, answered briefly, prayed simply, left.

" 'I was moved. I was comforted. I hated to see him go.'

"Be supportive. Those who comfort must have a tender heart of understanding. They don't come to quote verses or leave a stack of literature. They come simply to say they care. Nor do they attempt to erase today's hurt by emphasizing tomorrow's hope. They are committed to the support, the understanding of the grieving. Few things heal wounded spirits better than the balm of a supportive embrace.

"A little girl lost a playmate in death and one day reported to her family that she had gone to comfort the sorrowing mother. 'What did you say?' asked her father. 'Nothing,' she replied. 'I just climbed up on her lap and cried with her.'

"That's being supportive.

"Be available. Everybody comes around the first day or two. But what about a month later? After the flowers? Or five months later? After the grass grows over the grave? Life, like the muddy Mississippi, keeps rolling along. Unfortunately, so do the memories of that little fella whose place at the supper table remains vacant. If ever the comforting hand of a friend is needed, it is then—when other kids are going swimming and snitching cookies

and riding bikes. Be committed to comforting later on as well as now. Your appropriate suggestions that will help them break the spell of grief (C.S. Lewis wrote of 'the laziness of grief') will help them begin again.

"Like Jesus with the sisters of Lazarus in the crucible of grief, be real (He wept), be quiet (He took their angry rebukes), be supportive (He was deeply moved), be available (He stayed by their side). No big sermons, no leaflets, no attempts to correct their misunderstandings, not even a frown that suggested disapproval. Killing this giant takes time! Our Lord believed, as we should, that we are healed of grief only when we express it to the full.

"Perhaps this explains why so many are grieving and so few are comforting."[3]

WHAT'S YOUR PLAN?

God does have a purpose for the trials and testings that come into our lives. Here are several purposes of suffering or problems:

1. To draw us to Christ. God often allows circumstances to come into the lives of those who are not yet believers, so that they will come to Christ. Suffering shows us our need for God and forces us to turn to Him.

2. To prove God's sufficiency. We learn of God's sufficiency as we see our insufficiency. Read Jeremiah 17:5,7 and write your own paraphrase here:

In Psalm 91:14-16, what does God say He will do?

3. For our good and His glory. Read Romans 8:28. Does the "all things" include your circumstances, too? Read John 11:4. What was the purpose of Lazarus's sickness?

What does Hebrews 5:8 mean?

4. To draw us to the Bible. Psalm 119:67. What do you think this means for your life?

What did the psalmist's afflictions do for him (Ps. 119:71)?

5. To develop patience and endurance. Read James 1:2,3. How would you paraphrase these verses?

Romans 5:3. How is this possible (see v. 1)?

6. To minister to others. Read 2 Corinthians 1:3,4. Write your own paraphrase of these verses:

7. What does 2 Corinthians 7:9-11 mean?

8. What do these passages tell us God will do for us?
Psalm 28:7:

Psalm 31:24:

Psalm 40:1-3:

Psalm 121:

Isaiah 40:31:

Philippians 4:19:

Hebrews 13:5:

Notes

All material quoted is used by permission.
1. Gene Newman, Patrick Hamman, and Dorothy Clark, *All God's Children* (Redondo Beach, CA: ACAMPAR Programs, 1979), pp. 84,85.
2. Charles R. Swindoll, *You and Your Child* (New York: Thomas Nelson & Sons, 1977), p. 135.
3. Charles R. Swindoll, *Killing Giants, Pulling Thorns* (Portland, OR: Multnomah Press, 1978), pp. 39,40; Joe Bayly, *The View from a Hearse* (Elgin, IL: David C. Cook Publishing Co., 1969), pp. 40,41.

Parenthood Terminology
Test Answers

1. amniotic sac/fluid—the membrane and fluid which surrounds the fetus during the course of pregnancy.

2. Apgar score—a rating system for the newborn taken one minute and again five minutes after birth to see how well the child is adapting to its new environment. This system evaluates the infant's (1) color, (2) muscle tone, (3) heart rate, (4) respiratory effort/cry, and (5) reflexes at maximum two points for each area for a possible score of 10.

3. Braxton Hicks—periodic uterine contractions which may begin near the end of the sixth month. They have two functions: (1) to circulate blood, and (2) to strengthen the uterus for delivery.

4. cervix—opening through which the fetus passes from the uterus to the birth canal.

5. contractions—involuntary action of the uterus which accomplishes the stretching and pulling necessary to open the cervix. Contractions do *not* get stronger with each succeeding contraction. Some are stronger, others are weaker.

6. crowning—the first appearance of the baby's head at the vaginal opening, occurring immediately before birth.

7. dilation—the opening up of the cervix to allow the fetus to be

delivered. Opens to a maximum of 10 centimeters before birth.

8. effacement—the thinning out of the cervix, which occurs early in labor.

9. engagement—also called lightening. The settling of the baby's head into the pelvic bone readying the baby for birth; may occur up to four weeks before delivery.

10. episiotomy—a small incision which is made between the vagina and the anus to aid delivery and prevent tearing of tissues.

11. fundus—the upper rounded end of the uterus.

12. mucous plug—the blood tinged mucous plug which closes and protects the cervix's opening before labor. The "show" is the breaking loose of the plug before labor, or at the onset of labor.

13. placenta—the organ which is attached to the wall of the uterus and, by way of the umbilical cord, to the fetus through which oxygen and nutrients and wastes are exchanged between mother and child.

14. post partum—the period after the birth of a child.

15. transition—the period between first-stage labor and second-stage labor. Transition is the hardest part of labor but the shortest, occurring when the mother is about 7—8 centimeters dilated. Average length 1½ hours with first child.

ANF   Parenting/Family
          FBC #2714

Wright, H. Norman
Help, We're Having A Baby